"This new and very timely book is a real treasure. I highly recommend this book to everyone, especially to those who are presently undergoing that wilderness experience of deep hurt and trials. This is a book for our times, an important companion to our daily walk with God."

— PHIL KEAGGY
guitarist

"Michael is a humbled troubadour — an itinerant, a singing preacher — whose ballads are biblically rich, whose personal ministry is Christ-centered, and whose writings have but one intent: to bring glory to God by leading and feeding His children."

— HAROLD M. BEST
dean emeritus, Wheaton College Conservatory of Music; author of Unceasing Worship:
Biblical Perspectives on Worship and the Arts, *and* Music Through the Eyes of Faith.

"In an age characterized by triumphalism, it is hard to find biblically faithful meditations and songs on weakness, sin, lament, and suffering. Michael Card helps us understand the tears, while pointing us to the God and Father of our Lord Jesus Christ, and the comfort only he can give us, both in this life and in the life to come."

— DR. D.A. CARSON
research professor, New Testament Trinity Evangelical Divinity School

"A *Sacred Sorrow* is a refreshingly honest book about our dialogue with God and our life within the community of faith. The truths in it are absolutely liberating. It will not only change your prayer life, it will change every area of your life. I couldn't recommend a book more highly than I do this one."

— KEN GIRE
author of Windows of the Soul, Moments with the Savior, *and* The Divine Embrace

"Michael Card has lowered a bridge of lament across the moat of self-contentment and called us to weep in our fallen world, where only weeping can heal."

— CALVIN MILLER

professor of preaching and ministry studies, Beeson Divinity School, Birmingham, Alabama

"This book is written with a redemptive empathy for all who are hurting and helps us reconceive what it means to praise the Lord."

— CALVIN SEERVELD

senior member of philosophical aesthetics, emeritus, at the Institute for Christian Studies, Toronto, and author of Voicing God's Psalms

A
SACRED
SORROW

REACHING OUT TO GOD IN
THE LOST LANGUAGE OF LAMENT

MICHAEL CARD

NavPress®

A NavPress resource published in alliance
with Tyndale House Publishers, Inc.

NavPress is the publishing ministry of The Navigators, an international Christian organization and leader in personal spiritual development. NavPress is committed to helping people grow spiritually and enjoy lives of meaning and hope through personal and group resources that are biblically rooted, culturally relevant, and highly practical.

For more information, visit www.NavPress.com.

CONTENTS

PART Four: Jeremiah

PART Five: Jesus

PART Six: Conclusions

Acknowledgments

❖

Many scholars have helped me along this difficult path. Calvin Seerveld was the impetus for the start of the journey. Shortly after 9/11, I received a note from him in which he observed that we, in the American church, had no songs to sing in response to the horrific attack. The truth of what he wrote was self evident. "You need to write laments, to equip 'lament teams'," he said. I owe a tremendous debt to Calvin for that timely note.

Shortly afterward, on a visit to Trinity International University, Dr. Sun Myung Lyu, in a remarkable gesture of generosity, picked a book off the shelf in his office and handed it to me saying, "Receive this as my gift to you. I want to invest in your project." The book was Walter Brueggemann's *The Psalms, the Life of Faith*. That marvelous volume provided the foundation for my understanding of lament. Dr. Lyu, if anyone is encouraged by this present work, much of the thanks should go to you.

During that same visit, my friend Dr. Willem Van Gemeren also generously gave blocks of time to help get me started in the right direction. Later, Dr. D.A. Carson read the manuscript and helped me sharpen the theological focus. Their remarkable openness and the reassuring promise of their future help has made an enormous difference. I felt as if the safety net of their scholarship was always there. Thank you, brothers.

Dr. George Guthrie (Union University) has been a longtime friend and encourager, especially since Bill Lane passed away. His openness and willingness to join me as a conversation partner on this difficult journey has been a deep blessing. Thanks, George.

The writings of Ingvar `Floysvik and Michael Jinkins became primary resources and have helped so much to guide and shape the direction of this book. My gratitude to them for the enormous help provided in those volumes.

Most of all, I would like to thank Walter Brueggemann. His many articles and books not only shone a much needed light on this sorely neglected subject but they also provided a new vocabulary for thinking and talking about what is true of lament. His unique words and creative phrases will appear and reappear in this manuscript. I have sought to place them in quotation marks to show they are not original. His thought is present on nearly every page as is my gratitude to God for him.

As I was beginning in earnest to work on the rough manuscript, after having read many academic books and technical articles on the subject of lament, I picked up a remarkable book entitled *A Fistful of Agates*. It had been sent as a gift by the author months earlier. I had intended only to skim through it. Hours later, when, in tears, I finally put it down, I was given a whole new appreciation for Bill Lanes' often repeated maxim, "Timing is of the Lord." The timing of the reading of Jane Wipf's book was perfect. I had done the background, academic work. It was intensely interesting and held together intellectually. But God wanted a fully engaged person to write this book. And so, by means of Jane's book, He gently led me through the experience of lament at a heart level (which is, of course, the only level it can genuinely be understood or experienced!). All this is to say, thank you, Jane, for what it must have cost you to write that book.

I do not know how to adequately thank Dr. Eugene Peterson for providing the foreword. All I can say is, it was a "hesed" type of experience for me.

I want also to thank Rachelle Gardner and everyone at NavPress for their commitment to seeing this book through to completion. Rachelle's dedication to excellence and gentle encouragement to finish the task gave the final form to this project.

Finally, I want to thank the many brothers and sisters in my community of faith in Franklin, Tennessee, who listened and encouraged as the ideas for this book were "simmering on the back burner." The Tuesday night study at First Missionary Baptist, the Wednesday night study at Christ Community, and the Sunday night home fellowship group helped enormously in the organization of the material. Thanks also to the men of the Empty Hands Fellowship, especially Scott Roley whose unqualified acceptance of every new idea was a great encouragement, and Mike Smith, who took the time to read the manuscript and help me find several places that needed "adjusting." To Ken Cope whose dialogue about the personal and "soulish" aspects of lament made this, I pray, a deeper and more helpful book. To everyone who supports the work directly, Barbara Emerson, Connie Morkel, Kevin Kookogey, Danielle Schouten, and Tifany Borgelt, blessings to you for all the long days. Thanks also to Ron Davis and Sam Judd for their encouragement on the road. We have lamented a lot together in the past several years, haven't we?

This book is dedicated to my wife Susan and our four children: Kate, Will, Nathan, and Maggie. The Lord has walked together with us through many lamentable losses, not the least of which are the large blocks of time we are apart when I am on the road. Thank you for not giving up, not letting go, and never "leaving the dance floor" till the music was over. If indeed we are called to lament in this present world, I am thankful that we have each other, our family, and that we are not alone.

This book is presented by all of us as a gift to the church.

Author's Note

Much of the Old Testament Scripture quoted in this book is from the Tanakh, a new translation of the Holy Scriptures by the Jewish Publication Society.

The translation has a marvelous clarity and reflects the richness of rabbinic scholarship.

FOREWORD BY EUGENE PETERSON

IT'S AN ODD THING. JESUS WEPT. JOB WEPT. DAVID WEPT. JEREMIAH WEPT. THEY did it openly. Their weeping became a matter of public record. Their weeping, sanctioned by inclusion in our Holy Scriptures, a continuing and reliable witness that weeping has an honored place in the life of faith.

But just try it yourself. Even, maybe especially, in church where these tear-soaked Scriptures are provided to shape our souls and form our behavior. Before you know it, a half-dozen men and women surround you with handkerchiefs, murmuring reassurances, telling you that it is going to be alright, intent on helping you to "get over it."

Why are Christians, of all people, embarrassed by tears, uneasy in the presence of sorrow, unpracticed in the language of lament? It certainly is not a biblical heritage, for virtually all our ancestors in the faith were thoroughly "acquainted with grief." And our Savior was, as everyone knows, "a Man of Sorrows."

A number of years ago my mother died in Montana. My brother and sister, our spouses and children, gathered and prepared for the service of worship in which we would place our grief for her death and gratitude for her life before God. As the first-born I was appointed to conduct the funeral. I lived in Maryland at the time and so except for our immediate family and a few old friends, knew almost no one in the congregation. I called the congregation to worship and led them in prayers. I began reading Scriptures — several psalms, Isaiah's strong words of comfort, Jesus' parting words to His disciples, Paul's architectonic Romans 8, John's final vision of heaven. I had done this scores of times over many years and always loved doing it, saying again these powerful, honest words that give such enormous dignity to death and our tears. While reading, the air now thin between time and eternity, without warning lament surged up within me. I tried to keep my composure and then just let it go. I knew I was making everyone uncomfortable but remember thinking, They get to cry so why not me? Why am I the only one not permitted to weep? I had read these same Scriptures at the burial of my father eight months earlier, and at that moment it came to me that my parents had always been ahead of me, a barrier against my own death, and now they were gone. I felt suddenly exposed, alone. I was next in line. I gave in and let the lament out in uncontrolled sobs. It probably didn't last long, maybe twenty seconds or so. I wiped my tears, got my voice back, and continued with the Scripture readings and the rest of the service.

The benediction pronounced, I ducked quickly into a small room just off the chancel. I didn't want to see or talk to anyone. My twenty-two-year-old daughter slipped in beside me. We sat together, quiet and weeping our own "sacred sorrow." And then a man I'd never seen before entered and sat down. He put his arm across my shoulder and spoke some preacherish clichés in a preacherish tone. Then, mercifully, he left. I said to my daughter, "Karen, I hope I've never done that to anybody." She said, "Oh, Daddy, I don't think you have ever done that." I hope not.

This is a magnificently conceived and executed book. Michael Card has saturated himself in the rhythms, music, and truth of our people-of-God ancestors and written a necessary book for all of us Christians (and there are many of us) who have lost touch with our native language of lament, this language that accepts suffering and our freely expressed suffering as the stuff that God uses for our salvation. At-homeness in the language of lament is necessary for expressing our companionship with our Lord as He accompanies us through the "valley of the shadow of death" and who leads us to be with Him in "dark Gethsemane."

It is also necessary as witness, a Jesus-witness to the men and women who are trying to live a life that avoids suffering at all costs, including the cost of their own souls. For at least one reason why people are uncomfortable with tears and the sight of suffering is that it is a blasphemous assault on their precariously maintained American spirituality of the pursuit of happiness. They want to avoid evidence that things are not right with the world as it is—without Jesus (and Job, David, and Jeremiah), without love, without faith, without sacrifice. It is a lot easier to keep the American faith if they don't have to look into the face of suffering, if they don't have to listen to our laments, if they don't have to deal with our tears.

So, learning the language of lament is not only necessary to restore Christian dignity to suffering and repentance and death, it is necessary to provide a Christian witness to a world that has no language for and is therefore oblivious to the glories of wilderness and cross. A doubly necessary book.

— EUGENE H. PETERSON

Professor Emeritus of Spiritual Theology, Regent College, Vancouver, B.C. Canada

PART ONE

✸✸✸

AN ANCIENT LAMENT

CHAPTER I

THE PATH OF SOVEREIGN SORROW

BEFORE THERE WERE DROPS OF RAIN, HUMAN TEARS FELL IN THE GARDEN, AND that was when lament began. In Eden, Adam and Eve enjoyed the unbroken Presence of God. It was immediate and intimate. His *hesed*, an untranslatable Hebrew word often rendered "loving-kindness," was a given, reliable as the fresh, newly created air they both breathed.

Then, in a moment when the Presence seemed somehow impossibly absent, in some forgotten corner of the garden, Satan, the Accuser and ultimate cause of all lament, called into question the *hesed* of God.

"Here is some wonderful, life-giving fruit that He does not want you to have," he, in effect, hissed at Eve. He longed to deceive the first couple into believing that in order to know God, they only needed to know and receive His gifts. The great lie was that God's gifts were all that He was. The temptation was to believe that if the gift could not be had, then it was somehow not really real and neither was God's love. Do these vile whisperings sound at all familiar to you? Do you remember ever hearing them in some dark forgotten corner of your heart?

When it seemed His Presence was absent, the Accuser accused God of acting in a way inconsistent with His *hesed*. After all, Someone who is truly loving does not keep good gifts from His children, does He?

"*Why* doesn't He?"

"*Where* is He?"

And so the bite was taken. But it was not simply the bite itself that caused the Fall and gave birth to the first groanings of lament from both creature and creation. The bite was only a consequent act of disbelief. It was the denial and doubting of God's *hesed* that led to the *dis*-belief that caused the two prodigals to be driven into the wilderness of His absence, never to return. It was bound up with the *mis*-belief that God was only the sum of His gifts and no more. All this flowing from the stubborn sin of *un*-belief.

As the two outcasts made their stumbling way out of the garden, the *hesed* of God caused an innocent animal to be sacrificed to make garments to cover the nakedness of the first couple, so they would know they were naked. By such sacrifices, their sins would be covered until the time when they would be washed away by a final torrential wave of *hesed* that would break down the hillside of Golgotha, as One who was Himself the Presence of God would cry out in lament.

The Presence that had always been (and sadly would have always been) palpable and immediate was altered, seemingly broken, and lament became the language of Adam and Eve, of you and me, and indeed of all creation (see Romans 8:22).

Hesed disbelieved.

Presence seemingly broken.

The lamentable journey began through Adam for all mankind. But the heartbreaking sorrow of the three (Adam, Eve, and God) was not and could never be beyond His perfect intention. It was a sovereign sorrow that fell upon the world, a wordless sorrow beyond our knowing. And as His loving wisdom does with all things, even and especially with our sin, God would redeem their disobedience and sorrow, transforming it by means of His *hesed* into a pathway back to the loving-kindness of His Presence.

It was a shadowy path that began outside the garden. It meanders through all our lives, inevitably leading us through the darkest valleys of our fallen experience. But we must never forget that it is a path, that it is going *somewhere*. There is a final destination somewhere outside the gates of a city.

But I'm getting ahead of myself for now.

As we make our way along the shadowy twists and turns of the way of lament, two questions confront us again and again. They are echoes of the experience of the first couple in the garden. If you dig deeply enough you will discover that one or both of them lie at the heart of every lament, from Job's to Jesus'. The two fundamental questions of complaint:

God, where are you? (Presence)

God, if You love me, then why? (*hesed*)

CHAPTER 2

A DIFFICULT HOPE

ALL OF OUR JOURNEYS, YOURS AND MINE, BEGAN WITH LAMENT, DID THEY NOT? Before we uttered our first breathless cries, our mothers lamented in pain giving birth to us, just as God had said would be one of the consequences of Adam and Eve's first doubting (Genesis 3:16). We were all ushered into a world in which the first sounds we heard were inevitably weeping — weeping for pain and weeping for joy, because the two are often linked more closely than we can imagine.

After a brief moment of flailing arms and legs, we were wiped clean, swaddled, and given the comfort of the breast. We experienced strangely familiar shadows of presence in the warmth of our mother's embrace, and deep inside our wordless infant intuitions we felt the comforting reality of her *hesed*. We sensed in her someone who would never leave or forsake us. We felt, radiating from her heart, a love that would never let us go. But these experiences would always be fleeting, fragmented, incomplete, interrupted, and so, ultimately unsatisfying. Neither her presence nor that of anyone else could ever replace the Presence and *hesed* we were created to know and inhabit, that inhabits and knows each of us. The rest of our lives would be spent trying to satisfy our deep hunger for them both. We often lean too hard on friends to provide them for us. We inevitably drain our spouses dry in a vain attempt to fill that eternally empty reservoir in our souls that only His Presence will ever fill. We were created to live with Him in a garden, and yet we awake every morning in the desert of a fallen world. So each of our lives are pulled along by these needs, by the grim gravitational pull of the Fall, along the sovereign path of lament.

A HARMFUL SILENCE

As we began to try to understand the shape of the world into which we were born, we would all soon experience the "shushing" of parents whenever we would inevitably erupt into the wailing of our first infant laments. Contained somewhere in the heart of these demands to "be quiet," beneath the sincere attempts at comforting, lay a level of shame and the inescapable message that we should not cry out, we should not behave in such ways; that wanting the comfort of presence and the assurance of *hesed* were really somehow selfish. At that frustrating moment we entered into the very human, fallen aspect of denial, which is the polar opposite of lament. As a result we grew up trying to control our tears and trying to help others control theirs, thinking in the midst of it all sometimes that we might even be able to control the pain. All our ulcers and neuroses unfold as an inescapable consequence. That single pathway through it all, the path of lament, became overgrown, lost, left off all our maps.

The bottom line: We are all born into a world we were not really made to inhabit. We were created *for* God, made to flourish in the comfort of the Presence of our Father within the warm context of His undeniable *hesed*. Now, in this fallen world, we are cut off from them both. Only the loving sovereignty of all-wise God could redeem such a hopeless situation. His solution? To use suffering to save us. To redeem our own suffering and most significantly to redeem all mankind, through His own suffering on the cross to pay the price for our sin. In order to turn around and move once more in the direction of God, we must find this path He has carved out. We must call out to Him in the language He has provided. We must regain the tearful trail. We must relearn lament.

There are examples of those who have faithfully followed this path before us. Their stories resonate in the Bible. It should be no wonder then that lament is so much a part of the fabric of the Word of God. The Scriptures are filled with lament. Every major biblical character, from Abraham to Paul, is heard praying their protests to God and sorrowing for their sin by means of lament. The complaints are eerily similar throughout the chorus: "Why do You hide Your face from me?" "Where are You, O Lord?" "If You really love me with an everlasting love (*hesed*), then why am I sick, why do my enemies triumph over me, why am I forsaken, what am I to do with my sin?"

Depending on which commentary you pick up, you'll read that from one-third to over one-half of the psalms are laments. With the exception of one psalm (88), each lament turns eventually to praise, revealing an important truth that has been lost; lament is one of the most direct paths to the true praise we know we have lost. In fact, lament is not a path *to* worship, but the path *of* worship.

> [There is] a time to weep.
> ECCLESIASTES 3:4, NIV

But there exists within American Christianity a numb denial of our need for lament. Some theologians go so far as to say these biblical laments no longer apply to us. And so the language of confession sounds stranger and stranger to our ears. It is heard less and less in our churches, and when it is voiced, rarely are our sins genuinely *lamented*. Through lament, we regain both a sense of awareness and a language to express the hopeless depth of our sin. We discover a way to enter the Presence and there experience the despair that comes as a result of unconfessed sin. After all, can sins be sincerely confessed until their lamentable-ness is deeply felt by us and submitted to God for forgiveness through the blood of Jesus?

Our inability or refusal to enter into personal lament betrays the fact that we do not recognize the depth of our sin. We stubbornly refuse to have our hearts broken by it. The only result is that our sins continue to break the heart of God. It is only after lamenting our sin that our eyes can be truly open to the glorious truth that we stand forgiven, with the righteousness of Christ, and realize that we are in the Presence of the One who has heard our cries with tender and sympathetic ears.

Apart from lament, you and I are robbed of our true identity before God. We remain unaware of the depth of our fallen identities as sinners and blind to the reality and depth of the costly forgiveness that is offered to us through Jesus Christ. Confession *is* lament for the sin that began in the Garden. The painful honesty confession demands is the fabric of all lament, as is the deep need for forgiveness and restoration to God's Presence. It is as if worship and confession are one holy fabric held together by strands of lament.

The laments of Scripture can help us relearn this lost language. Characters like Job, David, Jeremiah, and even Jesus provide us paradigms of lament. They all freely spoke the language of lament that in the end cost them so much. They demonstrated for us lives lived in the freedom of lament. This book is simply an attempt to look at their lives and listen to their laments. This is not a book about some new way to get what we want from God. Rather, it is a biblical exploration of the spiritual lives of four broken men who gave up all they ever wanted to discover what it was that God wanted most to give.

CHAPTER 3

WILDERNESS WORTH-SHIP

"THE LORD, THE GOD OF THE HEBREWS, SENT ME TO SAY, 'LET MY PEOPLE GO that they may *worship Me in the wilderness*'" (Exodus 7:16, emphasis added). It is one of those tiny phrases most of us unfortunately read right over. But, as is so often the case in Scripture, it is the small detail that unlocks the immense truth of what the passage is saying.

Moses had fled to the wilderness. He had encountered the burning bush in the wilderness. He had returned from the wilderness to Egypt in obedience to the call of God on his life. In his final warning to Pharaoh before the plagues were to descend upon and devastate Egypt, Moses, speaking for God, says, "Let my people go that they may worship me in the wilderness." The goal of deliverance is always worship.

We all know the outcome. Pharaoh stubbornly refused to let Israel go and thereby brought down destruction on his own people.

Two points need to be understood here. First, the purpose of their deliverance was so the people could worship. The object of their freedom was not simply their emancipation. The purpose was the worship of God. The second point, which is more directly related to our discussion, is the setting of their prospective worship, "in the wilderness." True worship begins in the wilderness. Praise is almost always the answer to a plea that arises in the desert.

There Israel would experience lamentable thirst. In the wilderness, the rock would be struck and water miraculously provided. (Exodus 16;

Numbers 20). In the desert, as their enemies were attacking, God told the people, "Stand still, I will fight for you" (see Exodus 14:14). In these and numerous other instances, it was powerfully (yet not convincingly, for them) demonstrated to the people what their God was worth. And that is the central issue of worship: What is God worth? In fact, the first primitive form of the word was "worth-ship."

In the wilderness the children of Israel discovered that above all others, He was worthy. He was the Father they wanted. He was the Provider they needed. He was the Mighty One without whose protection they would have disappeared in the desert sands as had so many other lost people before them. As they discovered His worth in the stresses and strains that only the wilderness provides, the Father hoped His chosen children would have ascribed to Him *worth-ship*.

The wilderness is still the place of worship. But for you and me it is not a matter of dunes and dry ground; in fact, it may be deceptively green. Our hunger and thirst are more spiritual realities than physical ones. The desolation we often experience involves our yearning for a more palpable feeling of the Presence of God. We need spiritual bread every bit as much as they needed the manna in the wilderness. Our deep need for Living Water is just as intense as any thirst their parched throats ever knew.

And so we look to the One whose coming incarnated for us the Manna, the Living Water, and the Presence of God. Jesus has entered into the wilderness of our wilderness and has found us, His lost sheep. He has provided everything we need and more. He himself is our provision. It is our most profound experience of His worth. He is the answer to that most basic question of worship. Jesus shows us what God is worth and so we ascribe to Him *worth-ship*.

But the power of these realizations only comes to light in that dim, blinding light of the wilderness, in the context of hunger and thirst for His presence; in those situations when we cannot feel His *hesed* for us.

Those men and women whose stories the Bible tells show us that these dark hungers can only be articulated in the language of lament. The brokenness of the wilderness, the perceived desolation, the sovereign sorrow that is only experienced there must always lead us either toward God and His Presence and sufficiency, toward the comfort of His *hesed* and the provision of His forgiveness or else away from Him for a time — for some, sadly forever. That crucial moment turns on the decision to either lament in His direction or to walk away, back into the silence of the denial of that hopeless desert.

> I ain't got weary yet
> I ain't got weary yet
> I been in the wilderness a mighty long time
> And I ain't got weary yet
>
> I been walking with my Savior,
> I been walking with the Lord,
> I been in the wilderness a mighty long time
> I ain't got weary yet
> (Early Negro Spiritual)

There is no worship without wilderness. There can be no worshipful joy of salvation until we have realized the lamentable wilderness of what we were saved from, until we begin to understand just what it cost Jesus to come and find us and be that perfect provision in the wilderness.

If, as you are reading this, you find yourself in the wilderness, realize that though you may not feel like it at the moment, you are in the very place where the Bible reveals that true worship can begin. If you're like me, you might also find that you have nothing to say from where you are, no words to articulate the depth of the dimensions of your hunger, thirst, disappointments, frustrations, guilt, or anger. If this is where you find yourself, then I would like to propose that you (along with me) are poised on the edge of a promising place. We need only to push on toward the discovery of what God would have us cry out, of what He commands as the appropriate response to what we find almost unbearable. I would like to propose that you and I need to learn what biblical lament is about. We should look into the stories of those whose lives and laments have been enshrined in Scripture to see what they said when they found themselves in the place you and I stand today.

CHAPTER 4

LOST IN A GREEN DESERT

I STAND IN THE MIDDLE OF A CONGREGATION ON SUNDAY MORNING. THE service has just begun, a "season" of worship. All around me people I know and trust "enter into" the experience of worship. Some hands are raised, but not all, since this is not a requirement in our congregation. Some eyes are closed. All around me are friends, faithful followers of Jesus, who seem to be able to go to a place I have not been, cannot seem to go. Twenty minutes later the worship time draws to an end. All I'm aware of is the aching in my feet and legs from having to stand up for so long. We all sit down in preparation to hear the sermon, the Word of God preached. It is my deep shame to admit it to you now, as it is my shame before God every Sunday morning, that when I finally sit down I whisper deep inside myself where I hope no one, especially God, will hear, "I'm so glad that's over!" Still aching, I collapse into the pew. I feel as if I've been wandering alone in a desert. It is that particular kind of acute aloneness which is only experienced in the midst of a crowd. The desert is paradoxically green, made verdant by the worship of others. I feel cut off in the midst of those with whom I share the intimacy of the same indwelling Spirit. I remain frustratingly thirsty while those around me rejoice and drink in Living Water.

For years, since the early days of the Jesus Movement, I dealt with this shame by discounting those around me, calling into question the genuineness of their experience. I inwardly accused them of faking an intimacy with

27

Jesus that I could not believe was possible, simply because I had found it impossible. The older I get, the more I have come to realize that, besides it being a sin to sit in judgment on others the way I did, it simply was not true. Many *were* entering into a deep and genuine place of worship. It was my soul that was missing a piece that perhaps Jesus, in His perfect timing, has decided only now, all these years later, to grant me and perhaps, through this book, to grant you too.

Many of us these days find ourselves adrift in a sea of worship. For us it is a tractless green desert, and we can know neither the way through, nor what the boundaries might be. We fear the giants that might dwell in such a land, those unknown and unknowable fears of what could be. We fear the frightening possibility of the unlimited spiritual "success" of connecting with God. We fear what might happen inside us if we actually did enter before the throne. What sort of Person might we find there? An angry Judge? A stingy Benefactor? A disappointed Father? "Perhaps," we say to ourselves, "it would be better to remain here in the wilderness we know rather than risk trading it for an impossible garden we could never know."

So many of us simply remain, willingly, and willfully abandoned in this wilderness. We do not know where we are. We do not know where we are going. We even lack the language to describe our desolate place in this frustratingly verdant place. Bound by the personal sorrows and hurts we leave outside the door on a thousand Sundays, we are left to languish while those around us drink from a fountain that, to our eyes, looks dry. We are slaves to what we do not know. And muted by what we find ourselves unable to speak. We are thirsty. We are word-less and way-less. Our best hope of finding our way back to true worship lies along the pathway of lament, a path that promises to provide the only route through the green desert. If indeed we are lost, we must push forward together and take the land, refusing any longer to live as strangers there.

If we would only open the eyes that Jesus seems so intent on our opening, we'd see that what we thought was a desert is in fact our own homeland.

When the spell of the Fall is broken we realize we have been residing here all along, though not really *living*. Our souls knew the terrain. We spotted familiar landmarks all along the way. Our hearts understood better than we knew the various narrow pathways. We see that the fountain is indeed full to overflowing, inviting us to quench our sinful self-inflicted thirst.

Our failure to lament also cuts us off from each other. If you and I are to know one another in a deep way, we must not only share our hurts, anger, and disappointments with each other (which we often do), we must also lament them together before the God who hears and is moved by our tears. Only then does our sharing become truly redemptive in character. The degree to which I am willing to enter into the suffering of another person reveals the level of my commitment and love for them. If I am not interested in your hurts, I am not really interested in you. Neither am I willing to suffer *to know* you nor to be known by you. Jesus' example makes these truths come alive in our hearts. He is the One who suffered to know us, who then suffered for us on the cross. In all this, He revealed the *hesed* of His Father.

This same failure to lament also hampers us in being able to fully know and reach out to the poor, whom Jesus told us were to be our central concern. After all, how did Jesus come to know us but by entering into the poverty of our world as the "Man of Sorrows"? He lamented along with our experience of fallenness, though He "knew no sin." How can we speak to the suffering and poor if we do not learn their language, the language of lament? Until we learn to honestly embrace our hopelessness and theirs, there will be no true gospel to be heard. Until we learn to lament, we have nothing to say to most of the world.

It follows then, that if our refusal to lament separates us from ourselves and others, it also separates us from God. The heart of the issue after all is not really lament, it is God. What do we believe His character is really like? Is He merely a predictable theological entity who sits frozen on the throne, kept narrowly fenced in by our categories and definitions, safely far away from us like a lion at the zoo? Could that rigidly defined and depersonalized Deity ever be interested in our confusion and hurt?

Have we forgotten that the compassionate face of God was revealed to us in Jesus? Christ revealed to us the Father who stands in the road waiting for a glimpse of prodigal children returning to Him. Jesus revealed the One who gets up from the throne, forever motivated by His defining characteristic, loving-kindness (*hesed*). In Jesus we experience a God who is moved by our tears, who is even moved *to* tears. Until we learn to let our tears of lament flow freely in His presence we will never discover this deep dimension of Him. Only the Christ who became so familiar with our suffering can break apart that dispassionate dividing wall between ourselves, others, and God. Only the power of His tender tears can tear it down.

Perhaps, thus far, you have been in agreement. You have felt lost, have sensed a loss of your identity, have felt cut off from others and God, have discovered that you have even lost the language to communicate these deep feelings and a thousand more. So far so good.

"But," you inevitably respond, "Isn't it wrong to complain by lamenting to God? Is it not a sign of rebellion and faithlessness? How can it be appropriate to show my anger to Him?"

These are all fair questions. But let me do what Jesus usually did and answer your question with another question: Why then, does God enshrine so many laments in His Word? Laments, we must realize, *are* God's Word. Why are so many biblical characters shown as disappointed and angry with God? Do we seek to learn from all the other facets of their lives but this? I would put it to you this way. People like Job, David, Jeremiah, and even Jesus reveal to us that prayers of complaint can still be prayers of faith. They represent the last refusal to let go of the God who may seem to be absent or worse — uncaring. If this is true, then lament expresses one of the most intimate moments of faith — not a denial of it. It is supreme honesty before a God whom my faith tells me I can trust. He encourages me to bring everything as an act of worship, my disappointment, frustration, and even my hate. Only lament uncovers this kind of new faith, a biblical faith that better understands God's heart as it is revealed through Jesus Christ.

The Ultimate Test of Jesus

This leads us at last to Jesus. The most important test of any truth for every Christian can be put this way: Is this seen in the life of Jesus?

> You will weep and lament,
>> but the world will rejoice. You will be sorrowful.
>> (John 16:20, NKJV)

Again and again in the Gospels, Jesus pours out his heart in lament:
* when twice He laments for Jerusalem
* when He weeps Mary's tears at the death of her brother Lazarus
* when He experiences his final meal with the disciples and openly shares His anguish
* when He struggles with the Father in the garden of Gethsemane and His lament brings Him to the point of death
* when He endures the suffering of the cross and cries out word for word a psalm of lament.

Jesus understood that lament was the only true response of faith to the brokenness and fallenness of the world. It provides the only trustworthy bridge to God across the deep seismic quaking of our lives. His life reveals that those who are truly intimate with the Father know they can pour out any hurt, disappointment, temptation, or even anger with which they struggle. Jesus' own life is an invitation to enter through the door of lament. One warning: After we pass through that door, nothing can ever remain the same.

I hope to provide a biblical overview of lament in order to promote what Brueggemann calls this "difficult conversation" we are called in Scripture to have with God in that "dangerous place before the throne." It seems to me that we do not need to be taught *how* to lament. What we need is simply the assurance that we *can* lament; that and a fuller understanding of all that it can mean. I have tried to speak, as far as possible, not in technical or systematic terms but rather by means of the parables of the lives of the four central lamenters of Scripture: Job, David, Jeremiah, and Jesus.

A Lament: The Tears of the World

In any split second
There is enough pain in the world
To overwhelm every gentle heart combined.
The world's pain is as vast as the ocean.
The sorrow of the world is as deep as the sea.
Could the ocean really be the sum of the tears of the world?
>*Warm*
>>*Salty waves of grief*
>>>*A tidal force of sorrow*

That ebbs and flows as inwardly the world groans while outwardly its poor passengers cry out to a God whose eyes are dry.
When Jesus appeared there was a tear in His eye that was as old as the world. It was not His own. It was the world's tear.
And when even a single one of those tears would course down His unshaven cheek and disappear into His beard, it was as if a black breaker full of the world's tears was exhausting itself upon the clean sands of the shore of His Father's invisible compassion.
Jesus wept the tears of the world.
How is it my eyes are dry?
>*Or only wet with my own tears?*

For the tiniest speck of one of the millions of seconds of my life has there ever been the smallest drop of one of the world's tears in my eyes?
When they see me, does the world see a man of sorrows?
Or do they see a false pretended joy that they could never know because I have never known it myself? Could never know while holding so dear my own comforts.
Grant me, O Lord, an acquaintance with such tears that the world has wept.
Surely the presence of such a great grief in my life would displace my small sadnesses, my petty anger, my selfish sorrows.
O red-eyed Jesus, turn my tears into the world's tears.
And awaken in the deepest part of my falsely satisfied soul
One Vast Loud "Ekah!"[1]

— *Michael Card*

PART TWO

�֎✾✾

JOB

CHAPTER 5

THE DANGER OF DEFIANCE

A THOUSAND YEARS BEFORE THE MAN OF SORROWS WEPT, JOB BECAME
acquainted with all our grief. It is one of the most remarkable moments in
all the Old Testament, like a precious jewel lying just below the surface of
the soil we walk over every day. He had just lost everything, his possessions,
his cherished children. Learning of this unspeakable disaster, the Bible says
Job got up and tore his robe and shaved his head. Then he fell to the ground
in worship and said:

> Naked I came from my mother's womb,
>> and naked I will depart.
> The LORD gave and the LORD has taken away;
>> may the name of the LORD be *praised*.
> (Job 1:21, NIV, emphasis added)

So much is said about worship in our time. An entire industry has
grown up centered around it. But this sort of worship, this kind of praise, we
know nothing about. And so Job must become our first precious mentor of
lament.

The deep things of the faith we learn less by didactic principle and more
through people of faith and their simple stories. After all, the gospel is not a
systematic/theological presentation to which we give assent or not in order to

become "believers." No, it is a story, which we enter into even as it enters into us. We, in the most real and literal sense, become characters in this ongoing incarnating of the truth of the gospel. Its story continues to be told in and through us, and along the way we begin to understand.

I believe the same kind of incarnational process is at work in understanding lament. Eventually, when we are struggling to explain a difficult topic like prayer, faith, or perhaps servanthood, we resort to naming a person who incarnates that ideal. If we want to talk about personal holiness we inevitably speak of a Mother Teresa. When we seek to understand discipleship we think of someone like Deitrich Bonhoeffer, not because of his great book on the subject, but because his life and death validated everything he spoke about in his writings.

It is no accident then that in the Old Testament, before we enter the world of the Psalms, a world so full of lament, we must first be introduced to Job, who perfectly incarnates all the complex and contradictory elements of lament for us in his life. Only then will we be properly prepared to enter into the process of moving from Torah obedience (Psalm 1) to unfettered praise (Psalm 150), which Walter Brueggemann says is the journey of the Psalter. Job provides a primer of lament for you and me.

Each of the major themes upon which lament turns is perfectly portrayed in the ancient, ever new story of our broken brother from the land of Uz:

PRESENCE: Like all the lament psalms, Job's lament will center around one deep, central need — the Presence of God. God's perceived absence is the root of Job's whole problem, and only His Presence will finally answer the problem.

HESED: The root of every biblical lament involves an apparent violation of this defining characteristic of God. The one who laments in the Bible is giving voice, sometimes even accusing God of not acting in accordance to His own revealed character. This is certainly Job's quandary.

AUTHENTIC RELATIONSHIP: As in the other laments of Scripture, Job displays a brutal honesty that could have only been born out of a desire for a deep and genuine relationship with a God whom he believed could be moved by his tears. Job's God is not the same as the predictable theological entity worshiped by his friends. One of the truly exciting prospects of reading the book is witnessing Job's already close relationship being stretched and in the process becoming even deeper and more personal through the process of wrestling with God through his lament. Had Job entered into the denial of his friends, there would be no story.

FROM "I" TO "THOU": Another important movement we see in biblical lament is the exhausting of the self against God and the eventual turning back to Him. This is sometimes called the movement from "I to Thou." It is one of the more existential facets of lament. In faith, driven by guilt, fear, doubt, frustration, or even anger, I cry out to God. I give voice to my hurt, my complaint, all the black bitterness I hold against my enemy. This initial stage of lament is dominated with the personal pronouns, "I" or "me." At some unpredictable point in the lament, a turn is made. (We will look at this in more detail in part 3.) The self, exhausted of its emotional energy, seems to collapse into the Presence of the One who was there, seen or unseen, all along. This turning, which we will call "crossing the line," is powerfully portrayed in Job's experience.

FAITHFUL PRAYERS OF PROTEST: Finally, we see in Job one of the most fundamental lessons we will learn from lament: that the act of lamenting, protesting, and even accusing God through the prayer of protest is still an act of faith. Far from denying the existence of God, the lament of faith cries out on the basis of an appeal to the living God's loving-kindness, in spite of the fact that the present conditions would suggest otherwise.

In Job we discover a person who will simply not let go of God in spite of death, disease, isolation from friends and family, and ultimately a perceived abandonment by God. Those around him, including his own wife, plead for him to let go and die. But Job, like Jacob, faithfully holds on in the wrestling match of his life. And like Jacob, he no doubt limped for the rest of his faithful and God-haunted life. Once we witness his example, how could we ever expect otherwise?

CHAPTER 6

NEW LIGHT ON AN INCOMPLETE EQUATION

JOB IS CONTAINED IN A COLLECTION CALLED THE WISDOM WRITINGS
(Kethuvim), along with Psalms, Ecclesiastes, Proverbs, and the Song of
Solomon. (The Hebrew Bible includes several more books in this section
including Lamentations, Esther, Daniel, Ezra, Nehemiah, and First and
Second Chronicles.)

These so-called Wisdom Writings appear to have come together during a time of transition in Israel. The shift was not so much political or even
religious as it was existential. (I use the term "existential" not to describe
a philosophical point of view ["existentialism"], for indeed there exists no
such single unified philosophical position. I use the term in its pure sense of
describing something having to do with *existence* at its most basic level.)

From the beginning, Israel derived her understanding of the world on
what scholars like Walter Brueggemann call "Torah Obedience." This is the
basic understanding that if I keep the Torah, God will bless me, in fact He is
obliged to do so on the basis of His own Covenant. If I break any of His laws
He, by necessity, must punish me, as well as my descendants (Exodus 34:7).
This simple formula gave shape and meaning to Israel's world for centuries
and indeed is still operative in Judaism and unfortunately, in many Christian
denominations as well.

At some point in the history of Israel, no one knows just when, questions began to surface to which this simple formula seemed to provide no

answers. People, like Job, discovered that, even when they thought they had been "righteous" they still got sick and suffered losses. Israel sometimes felt this tension on a national level as well, most notably in the time of Jeremiah, when Babylonian "sinners" conquered God's people, the Jews. These questions, which confronted the centuries-old wisdom embodied in Torah Obedience, eventually found a voice in the Wisdom Writings. From this we see that the collection is not as much about wisdom as it is the perceived inadequacy of wisdom.

At the heart of it all, we see God preparing His people for a deeper understanding of Himself and His *hesed*. They will be invited to see that, though they had consistently broken the covenant, God nonetheless remained faithful and loving. It is more than they could have ever dreamed of or hoped for. This progressive revelation will find its fullest expression when He will send His Son, the Wisdom of God, to do for us what we could have never done for ourselves. He perfectly kept all the provisions of the covenant we had continually broken. He is the perfect High Priest who fulfills it all by sacrificing Himself, our spotless Passover Lamb.

Elsewhere in the Wisdom Writings, Solomon, the writer of Ecclesiastes, bemoans that though he was the wisest man on earth, wisdom was not enough. The Psalms, which we shall see begin with a hymn to Torah obedience, quickly pass into a series of laments which give voice to the growing frustration that there are inconsistencies in the fallen world to which Torah obedience provides no answer. Those who want a simple formula for their lives will not find it there.

This tension in the existential world of Israel is nowhere better seen than in the book of Job. Here is a man whose entire life was lived according to Torah Obedience. The narrator declares Job righteous in the opening chapter of the book (1:1). God Himself pronounces Job blameless in 1:8. The opening scenes show Job scrupulously offering sacrifices for imagined sins that his children *might* have committed (1:5). Eventually, God Himself declares that there is no one else on earth like Job when it comes to personal righteousness. If anyone should be a beneficiary of the ancient equation, it should be Job.

Into this simple, well-ordered world enters the Accuser. He twists and tangles the covenant promise of the Torah into a vile accusation. "Job," he hisses at God, "only loves You because he benefits from the equation. He is obedient because he gets something out of the deal. Take away the blessings and he will fold like a house of cards and curse You to Your face"(see 1:9).

God, who knows the heart of his gentle servant Job, knows that He is not loved by Job merely for the blessings or the benefits. So He allows a painful mystery to begin. "He is in your hands," the Father sighs. And Job's ordeal, and ours, begins. The book does not represent some sort of test whereby God might discover whether Job will be faithful or not. Clearly, His omniscience knew Job would never let go.

Job loses everything: his possessions, his children, and eventually, his health. At this point, to die would paradoxically be a blessing to him, but death is mysteriously denied him (6:9). The man of Torah obedience is forced to a painful place wherein he realizes that, though he might not have seen it by any other means, indeed he does love God for Himself and not simply as the source of all His blessings. The reason to love is not found on the other side of the equal sign of the equation. It is found in inequitable, untranslatable *hesed*. Without the pain, Job might have never realized either the depth nor the dimension of this kind of relationship with God, and perhaps never would we.

Enter Job's friends, the stewards of the old equation. One of the unexplainable mysteries of the book to me is their sympathetic week-long silent weeping session with him (Job 2:11-13). This wordless compassion leads us to expect more from them than we eventually see.

Though from slightly different perspectives, they all represent the incomplete equation of retributive justice. In the face of Job's experience there can only be one inescapable conclusion: Job has done something dreadfully wrong to deserve such suffering.

Eliphaz says, "What innocent man ever perished?" Conclusion: Job must not be innocent. As a consequence, Job has found himself clearly outside the protective hand of God.

Bildad says, "If you are blameless and upright He will protect you." "Surely God does not despise the blameless. He gives no support to evildoers." Conclusion: Job must not be upright.

Zophar says, "If there is iniquity in you, remove it!" The "if" says it all. If only Job will remove the sin from his own life, this suffering might all be over. The missing piece of the equation will reveal that it takes more to deal with sin.

Even young Elihu, from whom we hope for so much, flatly says, "He pays a man according to his actions" (see 34:11; 36:11).

Their one-dimensional conclusions are inescapable. Job is in the process of perishing for something he has done. There is no mystery, only the cold, hard reality of retribution.

In the course of this long theological exchange with his friends, the fatal fallacy of the old equation becomes blindingly clear: Is it within any of us to remove the sin from our own lives and live out a righteousness that could satisfy God's perfection?

In the book of Job we see that God is in the process of revealing the rest of the equation. According to Elihu, God pays man for being good, which echoes alarmingly the Accuser's accusation in Genesis 1:9. According to Satan, it was not love but only the payment of blessings that motivated Job's obedience. Through his allegation we see Satan's attempt to negate and steal Job's love away from God.

The heart of the complete equation, which only Job's suffering could have given him the arithmetic for, involves a God no one could have possibly imagined before, a God who pays the price for sin with Himself.

How does Job maintain his sanity, his ancient faith, through all the turmoil? By what means is he able to hold on to his hope, to his God, while the first notes of the song of this impossible completed equation begin to resonate? The answer: by means of the counterpoint of another song, the song of lament. Lament keeps the door open, keeps Job on the dance floor with God till the music is over, until the two tunes are resolved. The frustrated outpouring allows him to stay in the ring while everyone on the sidelines shouts at him to throw in the towel. By the end of the book, I always imagine Job and God standing with their arms around each other like a couple of weary boxers. Job's jaw is swollen. One of his eyes is black. He must keep one arm around his Opponent in order to remain upright. But he has a grin on his bloody face that comes from the knowledge that it was never about winning the fight. It had absolutely nothing to do with being right. It was always, only about being faithful. Job has survived the prescribed number of bouts. He has finished his race. His reward? Does he get his children back? No, he gets God back.

After this momentous confrontation with God, we do not hear Job repenting for his sin as much as for his old misconceptions about God (42:1-6). His three friends are charged by God of "not speaking the truth about Me." Their sentence: to ask Job to pray for them to the God he knows (42:7-9). They will receive forgiveness not as a result of the accomplishments of their personal righteousness, but solely because of the forgiveness embodied in Job's prayer and God's *hesed*.

The God of the completed equation is a God who is beyond all equations. He is wild and impossible and totally Other. Unknowable. That is what chapters 38 through 42 in Job are all about. But He is also gentle beyond our imagining and available beyond our wildest dreams. (He would someday dwell inside us!) The Unknowable One, whose Name could not be uttered, will someday have a face and a name and He will be called by that name by all those who love Him. And, with their own eyes, they will look upon the light of that face. Underneath all the blood and sweat of the book of Job lies the exhilaration of this future moment.

> I know that my Redeemer lives,
> and that in the end he will stand upon the earth.

And after my skin has been destroyed,
    yet in my flesh I will see God;
I myself will see him
    with my own eyes.
    (19:25-27, NIV)

CHAPTER 7

A NEW AND TRUER WORSHIP

EVERYTHING A PERSON COULD IMAGINE LOSING, JOB LOST. HE WAS THE TARGET of practically every sort of pain and loss a human being can know. He was the successful businessman who experienced sudden and total financial ruin. He was the AIDS patient, hopeless and beyond all cures, full of sores, abandoned by his friends. He was the victim of a senseless terrorist attack. He was the parent who lost not one, but all his children in one unthinkable catastrophe.

As the intensity of these torments crash down upon him in progressive waves, Job deals with the sorrow as best he can in varying degrees.

The first messenger tells of the loss of some of his livestock and the servants who were attending them due to an attack by the Sabeans.

The second messenger tells of what appears to be an attack by God Himself. The "fire of God" has fallen from the sky and killed the sheep and more of his servants.

The next messenger tells of the Chaldeans' attack on Job's camels and of the execution of still more of his servants.

The book speaks of no response from Job upon hearing any of these dreadful reports. Apparently he was able to cope with these losses somehow on his own. Job has felt the enmity of the Sabeans and Chaldeans before. Even the "fire from God" that struck his sheep . . . certainly natural disaster was nothing new.

But then the final messenger comes with an unthinkable message. A mighty wind had blown in from the desert, striking the four corners of one of the homes of his children. They had all been together at one of their frequent celebrations. No building could have survived such an assault, a wind striking from four directions at once. They are, all of them, dead.

How could Job find it in himself to "deal with" this final message? The answer is simply, he could not. He could see in his mind's eye each of his precious children lying there in the rubble. In the split second flash that only the human brain can create, he saw them all as infants, learning to walk. He could hear the stammering of their first words. He remembered them growing to adulthood, getting married, having their first children. He could see it all, could see them all, each one of their precious faces. And now they were simply gone.

It is vitally important to really hear the first two words of chapter 1, verse 20. They say it all. "*At this*," it reads, Job got up, tore his robe, and shaved his head. These were the prescribed, cultural things he knew and could do without thinking in his numbed state. They would have been expected of him by his community. For the lack of a better term, Job made the motions of entering into mourning.

What he does next, however, is totally unexpected, even unimaginable. Until this moment nothing remotely like it has happened in the Bible. Till now Job has responded as he should have, as he was expected to respond, as you and I would probably respond. What he does next seems unthinkable, almost impossible.

"Then he fell to the ground *in worship*."

That response alone determines the rest of his experience in the book, both good and bad. It must have been that aspect of his spiritual life that had caused God to boast about him in the throne room scene in the first place. Job is the sort of man who will simply not let go of God. To him, this is what worship means. He will stubbornly cry out in the groanings of this lament, which *is* worship until God answers. As Brueggemann would say, he refuses to leave the dance floor until the dance is done.

Because Job had the audacity to worship God in the midst of such indescribable pain, Satan will step up the attack with ferocious intensity. This time the battlefield will be Job's unfortunate body.

The tone set by 1:20 is the key note that must inform our reading of all of the rest of Job's story. It is not theology or theodicy, but a note of genuine grief, the depth of which few of us will ever know.

In the least it is inadvisable, at most impossible, to reduce the laments in the book of Job to a simple outline. Though, as we shall see, there are forms within lament, it follows no preset or predictable formula. There are roughly, however, five focused songs of lament that we hear from his lips.

3:1-26. After their week-long silent retreat is over, after he has had all that time to ponder the alternatives in his mind, Job has concluded that he will curse the day he was born. If only he had died at birth, none of this would have ever happened. He would have blissfully gone to wherever it is that infants who die at birth go. (Job's uncertainty about life after death and heaven is one of the indications of the great antiquity of the book.) This self-curse is really a form of emotional suicide. Though he is not "suicidal," it seems painfully obvious to him that it would have been better if he had not been born.

6:1–7:21. After Eliphaz's reproof, Job erupts once more in lament. Though Eliphaz seems to believe that such language directed toward God is inappropriate, indeed blasphemous, and a clear indication that Job is a sinner after all, Job refuses to let go of God. "Let Him crush me," Job cries out. In the desperate intimacy that can only be articulated through lament, Job addresses God by an incredible new name, "You." A foundational concept in the Wisdom Writings is that fear of the Lord is where true Wisdom begins (Proverbs 1:7; 2:5; 9:10). But that statement begs the question, "what is the end of Wisdom?" The chasm caused by the righteous fear of God is bridged by lament. As we cross over from fear to love (which must be the true end) we have on our lips a new name for God, the costly form of direct address, "You."

10:1-22. After engaging Bildad in a debate over the central issue of retributive justice, Job renews his insistence on his own innocence. "I know I am not guilty," he says.

13:17–14:22. Finally, exhausted by the nit-picking of his friends and the silence of God, Job goes to a place that most laments inevitably go. He laments the absence of the presence of God: "Why do You hide Your face from me?" Jesus will echo the same dark lament from the cross.

29:1–31:40. Job has endured the criticisms and insinuations of his friends for long enough. This, his final lament, reflects the tone of his exhaustion. In spite of his friends and their tiring theological arguments, Job still struggles to keep one swollen eye on God. He grapples to hold on to Him, not as a topic of discussion, but as his last reason for hope. "God has disarmed and humbled me," he moans.

We must never lose sight of the fact that all these laments flow from that first faithful response in 1:20, "Then he fell to the ground *in worship*." They are all connected to that initial act of worship by the threads of lament that weave together the fabric of the entire book. Job stubbornly insists on maintaining the dialogue with the God who, for a while longer, remains infuriatingly silent. He continues to offer up to Him all his suffering, his suicidal groanings, his confusion and hurt, even his own deep disappointment with God. He has come to the desperate understanding that there is no other place to take them but to God. They are the only offering he has left. He cannot lose now because he has nothing left to lose. Despite his heartbroken and heartbreaking accusations against God — that He no longer sees nor cares — Job sees with a crystal clarity provided by suffering that he simply has no place else to go.

Today we would ask Job to leave all these negative emotions at the church door. They are not appropriate to nor do they fit inside the narrow confines of our definition of worship. And so, likewise, those of us who have nothing else to offer but our laments find the door effectively closed in our faces. It cost Job everything to teach us this lesson. It is time we learned it.

Worship is not only about good feelings, joy, and prosperity, though they are at the heart of it. If this were true, then according to this modern American understanding of worship, the poor have nothing to say, nothing of value to bring to God. While Jesus would pronounce a blessing on those who mourn, we pronounce this curse. Those who "labor and are heavy laden" can find no place in our comfortable churches to lay their burdens. We reason, "Who could possibly conceive of a God who would want to receive such worthless empty offerings?" But Job desperately clings to such a God, one who encourages us to offer everything to Him, every joy and every sorrow. All our broken hearts. All our contrite spirits. Because He is *worth* it.

CHAPTER 8

THE FRUSTRATED LAMENTER

NOT A SINGLE VERSE OF THE OLD TESTAMENT FORBIDS LAMENTING. IN FACT, later on Jesus will bless those who do (Luke 6:21). One of the most helpful aspects of the paradigm Job provides us as a "lamenter" is the picture of his frustrated attempts to reach out to God despite the protests of his well-meaning friends. When we read the book of Job we are usually trying to decide who is right. Better to understand Job as a person who seeks to lament but who is interrupted again and again by his well-meaning friends. His heart tells him to go to God with his prayers of complaint. Our hearts tell us the same thing. Indeed, none of us need to be taught how to lament. What we need to hear is that we *can* lament.

As the frustrating conversation continues between Job and his friends, as they parry back and forth between their theological condemnation and Job's righteous indignation, a subtle erosion begins to take place in Job's faith.

When he enters into his suffering it is with a blessing for God on his lips (1:21). After his health falls apart, Job asks his condemning wife, "Shall we accept good from God, and not trouble?" (2:10, NIV). Anyone who has come to this place will tell you this is a costly understanding. To say in essence, "Whatever comes my way, I will not let go of God," reveals a heart that can accept suffering as the undecipherable mystery that it is.

After the arrival of his friends and their week of silence, the onslaught begins. Job will incessantly seek to cry out in lament to God, whom, as we have seen, he occasionally will boldly address as "You" (7:17-21; 13:17–14:22). In addition to their insinuations that Job is suffering because of his sin, his friends try to "shush" Job's lamenting. According to their belief, such a conversation with God is blasphemy. This follows logically from their view of a God who is bound by the narrow equation of retribution. Would not such a God take vengeance on the arrogance of a person like Job who challenges Him to His face?

"You subvert piety and restrain prayer to God," says Eliphaz (15:4). "That you could vent your anger on God and let such words come out of your mouth."[1]

But early on Job insists, "I will not speak with restraint. I will give voice to the anguish of my soul. I will complain in the bitterness of my soul" (7:11). "I insist on arguing with God" (13:3).

GOD, THE TOPIC

Job desires to struggle by means of lament to God. He sees no other way out of the wilderness of his suffering, as indeed there is no other way out. His friends, who cringe at the apparent blasphemous passion of the language of his prayers, shift the conversation subtly in another direction. They begin to talk *about* God. He is reduced to a subject they would have Job believe they understand. Their discussions *about* God incessantly break up Job's laments *to* God. The subtlety of the shift is disturbing.

After Job's second lament (6:1–7:21), Bildad responds with the language of retributive justice, the initial equation again. Job almost seems to be caught off guard, and in 9:1-35 he leaves his lament and begins to theologize against his narrow notion of how God works in the world. What seems most significant to me is not the intellectual progress of their argument but the simple fact that Job is being distracted away from God. He does not return to lamenting to God until chapter 10. Then Zophar appears and the same process happens all over again. Before he returns to his important and difficult conversation, Job has to reason with Zophar (12:1–13:16). Again, he has stopped lamenting, and God is slowly becoming merely a topic of theological discussion, no longer the One to whom he was so desperately reaching out.

Eventually, however, Job limps back to lament in chapters 13 and 14. It is here that Eliphaz pronounces the most forceful diatribe against Job's lamenting. At this moment, Job tragically gives up his lament altogether. From now on we hear only the lengthy responses from Job to their arguments.[2]

When he stops lamenting, Job ceases to reach out to God. He stops worshiping, no longer able to see that God is worthy to hear his case. What happened to Job happens to many of us who come to such desolate places: despair. Kierkegaard rightly called it "the sin that leads to all other sin." Though it may seem profoundly counterintuitive, lament and despair are polar opposites. Lament is the deepest, most costly demonstration of belief in God. Despair is the ultimate manifestation of the total denial that He exists.

Listen to the despair in Job's voice now as he moans, "Would that I knew how to reach Him" (23:3).

"He is not there." (23:8)
"He is hidden." (23:9)
"I am terrified in His presence." (23:15)

Not until 30:20 will Job attempt to cry out directly to God one last time. By then everything seems to have changed. The fight has all but gone out of him. All he can mutter is "I cry out to You, but You do not answer."

WHAT FRIENDS SHOULD WE FEAR?

Could it be that Satan, having seen that death and disease would not be enough to force Job to let go of God, sent Job's "friends" armed with an even more insidious weapon to attack him? Despair?

Job's distraction should serve as a serious warning to all of us. His friends were wrong about God. God Himself will say so (42:7-9). But Job was wrong as well. He was wrong to be distracted, to take his eyes off the God he could not see and focus instead on his rationalizing friends. He was wrong to give up talking *to* God and resort to dialoguing with them *about* God. It was as close to the brink as Job ever came. But Something seems to have held on to him in those last desperate minutes when he could no longer hold on for himself.

Job calls out to those of you who are in the wilderness, "beware!" It could be that your undoing will not be caused by the death or the disease, by the cancer or the failed marriage. Your worst enemies could very well be disguised as your friends. This is how to know the difference: Your true friends will be willing to sit with you in silence not for a week, but for as long as it takes. Your real friends will encourage you to keep talking, crying out to, arguing with God. And when you would be tempted to despair and quit the dance floor, saying that you simply lack the strength or the faith to go on, it is only your real friends who will have the love to leave you all alone with the One who desires, above all, to finish the dance with you.

CHAPTER 9

THE EXHAUSTED MYSTIC

MOST COMMENTARIES SAY THE STORY OF JOB IS ABOUT THEODICY, THE "problem of evil." I disagree. The book of Job is really about the problem of God! Or to put it another way, the mystery of God.

Were it not for the appearance of God in chapter 38, the book of Job would more resemble one of Plato's Dialogues than a book of holy Scripture. Until He appears, we only have bits and pieces, the fallen fragments of human theology and logic intermingled with the passion of Job's intermittent and failing tears. God's appearance at the close of the book is what sets it apart. His "showing up" is what the story is ultimately about. While much of the book concerns itself with the faithfulness of Job, who holds on; in the end the book is more a celebration of the faithfulness of God, who "shows up."

As so often happens, God does not make His appearance until Job's fingers have almost let go. It is a last minute advent, an arrival "in the nick of time."

As we have seen, the wisdom books are really about the inadequacy of human wisdom. By the conclusion of Elihu's final speech, you sense that you've reached the end of human wisdom, and if anything luminous is going to be said, it will have to be said by God.

If He had appeared in such a way as we might have expected, He would not be God; for God is always *beyond* and *unexpected*. Job has been crying out for answers. We would have expected an all-wise being to appear and answer all Job's questions, and ours. Job's friends have gone on and on about an outraged

Judge. If they had gotten what they were looking for, God would have appeared and condemned Job for his faults. But no one gets what they want, and when God finally appears, it is neither as judge nor answer-man. God arrives on the scene full of questions, and they are infinitely difficult questions!

The first one would have sufficed to shut them all down: "Where were you when I laid the earth's foundation?"(38:4, NIV). But what follows is a barrage, a train wreck of unanswerable questions. When their roaring echoes away like the thunder, all we hear is Job's amazed stammering, "I put my hand over my mouth" (40:4, NIV).

Then the sky opens up once more with another torrent of impossible queries. As if they weren't enough, God begins to sing two powerful songs, the song of Behemoth (40:15-24) and Leviathan (41).

Has anyone ever been more overwhelmed and exhausted than was Job when he came to the end of all this? His possessions gone. His children dead. His body ravaged by disease. His mind unraveled with who knows how many hours or days of argument and debate. Having come to the brink of despair, what emotional strength could he possibly have left? And after all this, what withering effect would withstanding such an onslaught from God have on such a beleaguered person? All this because of a dialogue between God and Satan about which he knows absolutely nothing! Only one thing can be said with any certainty about Job at this point:

Job has nothing left.

He takes his hand away from his parched lips long enough to whisper, "I spoke of things I did not understand, things too wonderful for me to know" (42:3, NIV).

These are the words of an exhausted mystic, of a man who has come to know that God is beyond all our words, beyond every equation. He is totally "other," completely uncontainable. And yet still, inexplicably, He showed up in the end. He came and finished the dance with the servant about whom He had boasted. Job, the prosperous patriarch, is now the penniless, broken man of lament. He has nothing left — but God.

"My ears had heard of You, but now my eyes have seen You!" (42:5, NIV).

A mystic is someone who has had an inexpressible encounter with God, an encounter with a Truth that cannot be described by words but can only become incarnate and seen, as Job has seen it.

We usually picture mystics as hermits or monks who willingly forsake everything for God. But all that Job lost had been violently ripped away from him. After all he had sacrificed, after all he had suffered, after all he had lamented, all Job gets back is — God!

The JPS translation renders Job's final words, "I recant and relent, being but dust and ashes" (42:6).

Having refused to let go through his stubborn lament, Job stands before God, broken, bloody, still covered with his detestable, putrefying sores. Having lost everything a person can lose, he now possesses everything!

In the end, the real miracle of Job is the spiritual intuition of Jesus he discovers through his pain and deep sense of abandonment by God. It provides a glimpse inside the mystery of just how God uses a false perception of His absence (for indeed, His very nature makes is impossible for Him not to be everywhere) to awaken in us the hunger for Immanuel ("God *with* us"). Job's realization of the incompleteness of the initial equation created in him a deep awareness of his need for someone to arbitrate between himself and God (9:33), someone he refers to as an Advocate (16:19), someone he calls Redeemer (19:25). Though his friends would dissuade him from reaching out through lament, Job holds on to the God he believes he knows, and is granted one of the most stunning images of Jesus in the Old Testament. Without the pain, he would never have known the need. Without the need, he would have never seen ahead to the One who will perfectly fulfill that need. The shadow of Jesus of Nazareth is there in Job. His prayers of protest are only a small drop in a sea of laments that would eventually call forth the coming of Jesus.

Though Job's suffering was not inflicted directly by God, He is always ultimately responsible. Job realizes in the end that he would have it no other way. God must be responsible if He is omnipotent, case closed.

So what are we to do with Him? What did Job, David, Jeremiah, and Jesus do? They simply refused to let go. Job perfectly prepares us for the coming journey from Psalm 1 to 150. As innocent sufferer, Job becomes a forerunner of Jesus. His life whispers the truth that would be shouted from the housetops of Jesus' experience; that only suffering can save us. Job is a ramp leading up to the "man of sorrows."

(Now would be a good time to put down this book and go read through Job. It will take the average reader a couple of hours to do so. As you read, look for the progression in Job's experience as a frustrated lamenter. Try to read at the level of your own imagination, seeking to enter into and share Job's frustration. When God appears at the end of the book, make an effort to understand what it would be like to attempt to answer that long line of impossible questions!)

> *A LAMENT:*
> *O Lord,*
> *In the sacrament of this moment*
> *Let the wordless sorrow of my silence . . .*
> *Give voice to my praise of You.*

PART THREE

✳✳✳

DAVID

CHAPTER 10

Hunger-born Songs of Intimacy

From the beginning, David was no stranger to pain. And in the end, it was the process of lamenting his pain that led him to an unheard-of intimacy with God. From his pen flowed the intimate words of suffering that Jesus would one day use in giving voice to His own pain on the cross. Through the words of those laments, God would redeem a mountain of sin and spiritual suffering. Through his psalms of lament, as perhaps nowhere else in Scripture, David reveals a God who uses and utilizes everything, especially pain. All true songs of worship are born in the wilderness of suffering. It is the pen of pain that writes those songs that call us forth to dance. David, like no one else, suffered and danced throughout the stumbling course of the rocky terrain of his lonely life.

From the beginning, David lived a solitary life, cut off from the intimacies you and I take for granted. Before he even drew breath, birth order was against him: He was the youngest of eight brothers. The complicated dynamics of family that we are only now beginning to understand would have worked against the young boy. Children born first and even second tend to receive more attention and favor from their parents. Children born last, as was David, are listened to the least and tend to develop more than their fair share of emotional problems, such as depression. But our greatest strengths are always our greatest weaknesses and so, conversely, last-born children develop early in life a hunger for intimacy that can become either an asset or deficit, or sometimes both at once. Perhaps it is this interior hunger that causes more last-born children to be drawn to the intimacies of art and music. David, as we shall see, responded to this tug as well and at some point early in his life picked up the harp.

When first we see him, David is alone and forgotten, tending his father's sheep in, of all places, the wilderness. When Samuel comes looking for God's anointed, no one in the family considers David to even be a remote possibility for kingship. In fact, the lonely truth is, no one considers David at all. When we come to know his seven strapping brothers, we arrive at the distinct impression that, had it only occurred to them, they might have sold their younger sibling, just as Joseph's brothers had done some eight centuries earlier.

In Judaism, a rabbi purposely avoided talking to his sons about anything but the Torah until the boys were twelve years old. The reason given is, "so that they can learn to 'walk around inside themselves.'" Though his father, Jesse, was no rabbi, David knew the terrain of this interior wilderness and wandered there all his days.

What followed was a life of growing up in the wilderness, the emotional wilderness he experienced in the midst of his family but more significantly, the actual wilderness of the hills around Bethlehem, a deserted place which would later shape the boyhood of Jesus.

Fifteen stories come to us from the Bible of David in the wilderness. There he faced his bitterest enemies, among them Goliath and the Philistines (1 Samuel 17). He came to know death on a scale you and I can scarcely imagine (1 Samuel 27:9; 2 Samuel 8, 10). In the wilderness we are told he would, "[weep] aloud until he had no strength left to weep" (1 Samuel 30:4, NIV). When later he would lament, "my soul thirsts for you . . . in a dry and weary land where there is no water" (Psalm 63:1, NIV), David's words sprang from a thirst for intimacy with God that could have only been shaped by the desert-desolation of the wilderness. It was there he learned how much he needed God. It was there he learned God's worth and so it was there he learned *worth-ship*. This was the obscure beginning of an intimate relationship with God that would give shape and meaning to his life, his kingship, and eventually the life of a nation.

The wilderness-born gift of hunger for intimacy with God is echoed in all our yearnings for relationship as well. Sometimes it leads us away from the Source and we look to others to fill that God-shaped place in our souls. At one point in his lonely life David sought such illicit intimacy from Bathsheba, and the consequences almost destroyed him. But God, who uses everything, can use even illegitimate longings to draw us eventually toward more legitimate relationships. Here we experience finite reflections of a deep satisfaction that only knowing Him can provide. David found such reflections in his intimate friendship with Jonathan.

By rights, they should have never been friends in the first place. After all, the throne should have gone to Jonathan, the son and heir of Saul. If ever there was a genuine reason for jealousy, Jonathan possessed it in spades. But Jonathan seems to have been deeply repulsed by his father's hatred for David. He witnessed its poisonous results and determined that he would not follow the same dark path. What he offered to David was precisely what Jesus would command from His followers a thousand years later: enemy-love, another illuminating translation for *hesed*. Indeed, when David later lamented the death of Jonathan, *hesed* was the word he used to describe the love they shared (2 Samuel 1:26). David had found a singular friend in Jonathan. But no friend, no soulmate, no spouse could ever fully fill the Divine dimensions that echo in our soul's need for intimacy with God, for His Presence, for *hesed*.

In the wilderness, the stark severity of David's life pressed him to make one of two choices: avoid the forsaken sense of suffering it causes and find a substitute for intimacy with God, or stubbornly refuse to let go of the loneliness and continue on the path toward an ever-increasing, continuously painful, unheard-of intimacy with God. David's two choices are still our only ones today.

A LIFE FASHIONED FOR LAMENT

THE WILDERNESS STRUGGLES OF THE LIFE OF DAVID BECOME THE MAJOR themes of his psalms of lament. As, time and time again, he was confronted with death and disease, David would flee to the comfort of his simple, ten-stringed lyre. As he felt the soft breath of the resonance of the strings on his fingertips, he found the words to cry out to the God he knew held the power over death. Out of the shadows of his solitary life, he discovered solace and a path back to intimacy with God through the laments he began to create and sing, no doubt, when he was a lonely shepherd boy. As he faced over and over again the frightening specters of the many adversaries life would hurl in his direction, lament would provide a bridge back to the safe Presence of God. An unheard-of hunger for *hesed* and a passion for Presence permeated the lonely life of the first shepherd king of Israel.

David's kingship began with a sad lament. However, it was not David who sang it, but God:

> "It is not you they have rejected, but they have rejected me as
> their king. As they have done from the day I brought them out
> of Egypt until this day, forsaking me." (1 Samuel 8:7-8, NIV)

When the people urged Samuel to anoint a king over them, God's chosen people, the prophet protested. Though God had chosen them, sadly, they refused to choose Him. In his old age Samuel had appointed his sons to be judges over Israel but they had failed miserably (1 Samuel 8:1-4). The people had had enough. To their worldly wisdom a human king was the only solution. Samuel did his best to warn them of their disastrous decision. A human king would end up enslaving the people. He would take their sons and daughters. He would take their fields and groves. He would take everything, in stark contrast to God who longed to give them everything! Samuel saw where it would all end:

> When that day comes, you will cry out for relief from the king
> you have chosen, and the LORD will not answer you in that day.
> (1 Samuel 8:18, NIV)

Rejected by His people, hounded by a hopeless sense of separation from the ones He loved the most — the Lord shared these feelings with His young shepherd king. David would lament them again and again to God, as God would lament them through David. Lament became a bridge between them. They would cross it again and again in their loneliness and find each other. God sensed in David's soul, as He would later in Hosea, something that resonated with His own loneliness and feeling of rejection. Perhaps it was the source of their deep friendship and the touching pledge that God Himself made to David (Psalm 89).

From the first moment we meet him, David's life seems more a fantasy tale than true. When God rejects Saul and sends the prophet-priest Samuel to anoint the unlikely boy king, the story could have come from one of Mallory's tales of Arthur.

In 1 Samuel 16, the prophet arrives and invites Jesse and seven of his sons to partake in a sacrifice. It is a ruse designed to keep them safe, since if the deranged Saul knew the real reason Samuel had come, none of their lives would be worth the few drops of anointing oil in Samuel's horn.

As Jesse's oldest son Eliab enters the tent, Samuel seems impressed by his stature. After all, the young man had already fought successfully with Saul and proven himself in the bloody rigors of primitive warfare. "This has to be the Lord's anointed," Samuel says to himself. "It all makes sense. He is the oldest. He is the tallest. He is the strongest. He is the most promising. This is the kind of man Israel needs."

The lessons contained in the Lord's simple silent interior response to Samuel could fill a library of books:

> "Do not consider his appearance or his height, for I have rejected him. The LORD does not look at the things man looks at. Man looks at the outward appearance, but the LORD looks at the heart."
> (16:7, NIV)

Jesse's other six sons will all be rejected as well, for though they are all strapping young men, God has looked upon their hearts and found them wanting. But Jesse has one last, perpetually overlooked son. His heart has been shaped in the wilderness, formed in lonely places. He is not the oldest, nor the tallest, nor the strongest. He seems, by far, the least promising of all Jesse's sons. He is decidedly *not* the sort of man Israel would think it needed as a king. Like a line from the prince's servant in Cinderella, Samuel asks, "Are these *all* your sons?"

Jesse shrugs his shoulders and sighs, not unlike the stepmother in Grimm's fairy tale. "Well, there *is* David," he says with a strong tone of incredulity.

David is sent for, the boy with the shepherd's staff and sling. His face is flushed for he has sprinted excitedly all the way back to the tent. After all, he is not used to being called for, only looked down upon.[1] Samuel produces his horn filled with anointing oil and pours it on David's small, tousled head. Amidst that simple, Bedouin backdrop, the Bible makes the ominous pronouncement, "From that day on the Spirit of the LORD came upon David in power" (16:13, NIV). No celebration. No coronation. No miracle pulling a sword from a stone. No, "long live the king!" Still, it was the beginning of a king who would "live long" but it would be twenty long, difficult years before he would take his God-given throne over Israel.

EVER-PRESENT ENEMIES

What follows is an account of the commencement of David's service to Saul, who in contrast to David's "Spirit of the Lord," was possessed by an "evil spirit *from* the Lord." At first the unstable Saul took a shine to David, but all too soon, out of envy, he would come to bitterly despise him. The first circle of David's experience, outside his condescending brothers, contained a man who would become his bitterest enemy, though David could never find it in his God-seen heart to hate Saul in return.

In the next concentric circle came Goliath and the Philistines. They were not the first, nor would they be the last in what would become a long procession of enemies. Paradoxically, David's great victory over the imposing giant would almost become his undoing. Saul's jealousy would flare. David would once more be forced to flee.

Enemies from within his family and his tribe. Enemies, giant ones, outside, all around. What followed was a life infested with such enemies and dominated by the struggle against them. Like a caged bird with broken wings, David responded with songs of lament, using them to transform his enemies and the hatred he bore them into worshipful offerings he made to God.

Only someone who is fully awake and engaged in life can lament. Lament only comes from the lips of those who know the hunger and thirst, the true terrain of the wilderness, the only place where worth-ship is realized. This lonely bridge can only be crossed by the one who has felt the depth of the chasm that must be crossed, the dark valley that exists between us and our lonely God, the one that exists between us and the lost and lonely men and women who surround us like dry dunes in the desert.

David's was a life that was indeed fashioned for lament. The truth is, all our lives are. Seen or unseen, we all have enemies that loom sometimes like

Goliaths on the horizon. We all are tempted to lose hope, to let go. We all face the enemies of disease and death. The terrible truth is we are, all of us, alone but for the One who waits on the other side of the bridge of lament. He offers not solutions, but only His Presence. Our tensions are rarely resolved, but as they are offered up we inevitably discover a new joy. He bids us to give voice to our confusion and disappointment, even as His own Word gave them a human, flesh-and-blood voice. If we would only join David in lament, we might discover that voice. We might discover as well (in the light of Jesus) that even as we cry out to God, we are crying out with God.

CHAPTER 12

ENEMIES AND "THE POISON WE DRINK"

WHENEVER A PROCESS IS MISTAKEN FOR THE FINISHED PRODUCT, THE RESULTS can be disastrous. Politicians are notorious for this. The worst of them continually promise conclusive, definitive results to their constituents. If we lived in a monarchy and they were kings, perhaps it might happen. But this is a representative republic and politics is a process. The most they can promise and indeed, what the best of them do, is commit themselves to the long and difficult process of change.

We understand sanctification to be a process as well. That is, God is engaged, through the Holy Spirit, in the process of making us holy. Those who see themselves as finished products usually become frustrated and disillusioned. Above all, they often enter into a deep denial. Sanctification is a work in process. We each are an unfinished product.

In Luke 6:27 (also Matthew 5:44) Jesus is describing the kingdom of God and the totally unorthodox *process* of its coming into the world. He makes an incredible, impossible, unheard-of demand on His followers. Luke tells us that before Jesus makes this difficult pronouncement, He looks directly at His disciples and, of all things, utters a rabbinic blessing on those who weep (or lament).

"But I tell you who hear me," He says, "Love your enemies, do good to those who hate you, bless those who curse you, pray for those who mistreat you."

What Jesus is doing in Luke 6:27 is extending the definition of *hesed* to include those who would take up their cross and follow Him. For one translation of *hesed* is "enemy-love." If only they could begin loving their enemies in this way, promises Jesus, they will become "the sons of El Elyon, because He too is kind to the ungrateful and the wicked." I am convinced that Jesus' next words could be translated, "Do *hesed*, just as your Father does *hesed*." Describing the same incident, Matthew 5:48 (NIV) says, "Be perfect . . . as your heavenly Father is perfect."

Love your enemies. Extremely difficult?

Love them the way God loves them? Impossible!

This is an issue that won't go away. Having broached the subject, Jesus will have to explain it again and again. He tells the parable of the Good Samaritan in Luke 10 to reinforce the point. He will go to the cross to drive it home.

It is an inescapable demand of following Jesus: We are called to love those who hate us, our enemies. No amount of theological backflips will ever free us from this impossible demand.

But then we come to the imprecatory psalms and what seemed an insurmountable demand before, now becomes contradictory and impossible. We call them the "imprecatory" psalms because they are laments that contain imprecations or curses. Some scholars debate whether these should even be included on the lists of laments at all. For our purposes we will include them for two reasons: First, they involve, in varying degrees, David's disappointment with God. That is, that He has allowed the enemy some degree of power over him to the point that David must cry out for help. Secondly, David's imprecatory laments represent a worshipful offering up to God of what would otherwise be considered an unacceptable offering: his hatred. Through lament in general, we bring to God our fears and frustrations, our pain and hopelessness. All these are seen by some (like Job's friends) to be "unworthy" offerings. God nevertheless encourages us in His Word to offer them up by means of lament. What makes the imprecatory laments

"laments" is that they represent our offering God the "unacceptable offering" of our bitterest hatred of our enemies.

From one point of view, Jesus' words and David's psalms of imprecation seem mutually exclusive. There are those theologians who say as much and are left in the embarrassing position of having to say that some part of the Bible is somehow "not for us," or does not apply. But how could such a thing be true? And if this is true, then who decides which parts apply and which don't? Others quote passages such as Ephesians 6:12 and conclude that now our only struggles are against what Paul refers to as "spiritual forces," and therefore these can only be considered as our legitimate contemporary enemies. But this only opens the door to denial.

If we are to love our enemies the way Jesus commands, we must first confess the fact that we have enemies. And here is where we come back to our original discussion of process. What we fail to understand is that Jesus is calling us to commit ourselves not to a one-time action but to a *process*. He has pledged His Holy Spirit to "come along side" in making this otherwise impossible forward progress a possibility. He has granted us His grace in making it an eventual reality. Here is precisely where David's imprecatory laments fit in.

When we look at the tumultuous life of David, it is no wonder that so many of his laments have to do with deliverance from his enemies; he had more than his fair share of them. In Psalm 35, David prays that the Lord will fight against his enemies, that they will be put to shame and dishonored. His enemies, says David, "gathered in glee" when he lamented. If only the Lord will "wake up" and defeat them then he promises, "my tongue will speak of your righteousness and of your praises all day long."

The Hebrew superscription to another lament, Psalm 58, calls it "a miktam," or script. The lyric is paradoxically set to a long lost melody entitled "Do Not Destroy." But the intent of the words could not be more different. Psalm 58 is a cold-blooded prayer for vengeance. There is a rabbinic tradition that says David wrote it in response to the events recorded in 1 Samuel 19, when Saul tried to kill him. Jonathan warned David instead, telling him to hide in a field. Perhaps while he was in hiding, before Jonathan's appeal temporarily softened his father's hard heart, David composed these black thoughts.[1]

"Break their teeth," he implores God.

"Let them melt away like a slug as it moves along."

And then comes an image you would expect more from the Taliban than David: "The righteous will be glad, when they are avenged, when they bathe their feet in the blood of the wicked."

It is difficult to believe that these thoughts could come from the same heart that penned, "The Lord is my shepherd." James, the brother of Jesus, voiced the same disillusionment in James 3:10: How could such beautiful blessings and cold curses flow from the same mouth? It should not be, he said. Indeed, James was right. They should not, but the sad fact is, too often they still do.

Psalm 109 (NIV) is as dark a place as exists in Scripture outside Golgotha.[2] It is never used for worship in Jewish liturgy. David's enemy appears to have been some sort of official to whom he had offered his friendship. Some scholars believe the occasion for the writing of the psalm was one of the many coups with which David struggled in the latter years of his reign. In the psalm, David says he has been lied to and attacked, and in return for his friendship, he has been accused.

Then David makes what at first seems an unremarkable statement, until you read the curses that follow. "But I am a man of prayer," he says in verse 4. What might we expect from a "man of prayer"?

> "Let an accuser (or the Accuser) stand at his right hand."[3]
>
> "May his days be few."
>
> "May his wife [be] a widow."
>
> "May his children be wandering beggars."
>
> "May no one extend kindness to him."
>
> "May he be cut off from the memory of the earth!"

The curses continue until David exhausts himself — his hurt, his hatred, and his anger. In verse 21 he gasps, "Out of the goodness of your *hesed*, deliver me." David is not yet repentant for his hatred of his enemies. He does not even seem to be capable of knowing how such a thing could be possible. All he knows is that he needs to be delivered from his hated enemy and from himself, and from the hatred he has for his enemy. In verse 26 he repeats the cry, "Save me in accordance with your *hesed*." David understands that as much as he needs to be saved from his enemies, the sin of his own hate is something he needs salvation from just as urgently. If he is ever to be saved from the pain and confusion in his life, he knows it will only be through the "unexpected love," through the "enemy-love" of God.[4]

Though David was a man who could respond in battle with a ferocious vengeance, what little we know of the historical backgrounds of these imprecatory laments would lead us to believe that he never took his revenge on any of those who were the objects of these often poisonous prayers of protest. By placing his enemies in the hands of God, David acknowledges that revenge is His alone (see Deuteronomy 32:41). Perhaps these psalms were the only thing that stood between David and the revenge he would have taken.

When his nemesis, Saul, finally commits suicide, David laments without an ounce of bitterness in his heart (2 Samuel 1:19-27). Even as he refused to let Saul's hatred of him shape his life, David would not let his own hatred of Saul stand in his way. There was nothing else David could do with his hate but take it to God. Prayer seems to have held no meaning for him otherwise.

We are a people in perpetual denial of the hidden hate we have for our enemies. Jesus showed us that hatred is a wound that must be healed, that denial is a paralysis only He can heal. Without lament these wounds continue to fester. The longer they are denied, the more gangrenous they become. These wounds demand that I answer the question: Is there any other way to handle my anger and hate but to bring them to God? Understand, imprecatory laments are not some sort of vicious didactic means by which we learn how to curse our enemies. They represent an invitation to the beginning of a process in which first, we admit that we do have enemies. Then these laments serve to guide us in the process of confessing our darkest hatred toward them with a view toward finally handing them over to God.

CROSSING THE LINE

Psalm 13 echoes with David's frustrated cry, "How long?" To David it seemed God had forgotten him forever, leaving him in the hands of his gloating enemies. This psalm is one of the best examples of the resolution that occurs in every lament psalm except one (88). It marks the transition from despair to hope, from complaint to praise. If we want to move ahead on our understanding of lament we must grasp this important facet.

In the Psalms, the transition is almost always marked by the English word "but" or "then," and reflects a Hebrew particle known as the "vav adversative." *Vav* is, in fact, the sixth letter in the Hebrew alphabet. (Another system of pronunciation renders it "waw.") It looks like this: ו — a short vertical line with a little flag on top that perpetually seems to indicate the wind is blowing from the east. It is generally used to join ideas and is most frequently translated "and." Sometimes it serves another purpose, to help express antithetical or "adverse" ideas. When used in such a way it is called the "vav adversative."

The transition marked by this upright line of a letter is always abrupt. It indicates that somewhere, somehow an invisible line has been crossed and the focus of the lament has turned from the self to Elsewhere.

Sometimes it seems simply a matter of exhaustion. I cannot bear the burden of my sin any longer. *I have no more tears left to weep. I have no more outrage left to voice.* At other times the person lamenting simply seems to wake up. In the course of his prayer of complaint, something jogs his memory and he calls to mind those past times when God was faithful, when He showed up in the nick of time and saved the day. It is the line that must be crossed from the sorrowful self-centered "I," "me," or "mine" passages to the praise-dominated "You" verses when it has been at last realized that God *is* faithful.

Like some sort of interior spiritual San Andreas Fault line, it represents the precise point where two continents have been rubbing up against one another — the huge island of self and vast uncharted and unknowable continent of God's Presence. It is the line of a momentous movement from "me" to "You." It is a signpost along the journey of the psalms, from Torah obedience (Psalm 1) to worship (Psalm 150).

Often, after this line is crossed, God is addressed by a new and revolutionary name, "You." The adversity delineated by the adversative leads to an unheard-of, borderline blasphemous, direct form of address. The distant God, enthroned "out there," has risen from His throne, moved by compassion, moved by our tears. The wilderness wasteland that is crossed by means of lament leaves the lamenter exhausted, only capable of falling into the intimate embrace of the one "You." We would have never known Him thus unless first, we had honestly wept; and second, turned from the self of "me" to the otherness of "You." Those who have been to this place know that it is the most remarkable place of rest, though it is an exhausted rest.

David has left us a masterpiece of this movement in Psalm 13. (Forgive all the bold type and italics. They only help to reinforce the point.)

> *For the choir director: A psalm of David.*
>
> O Lord, how long will you forget *me*? Forever?
>> How long will you look the other way?
> How long must *I* struggle with anguish in *my* soul,
>> with sorrow in *my* heart every day?
> How long will *my* enemy have the upper hand?
>
> Turn and answer *me*, O LORD *my* God!
>> Restore the light to *my* eyes, or *I* will die.
> Don't let *my* enemies gloat, saying, "We have defeated him!"
>> Don't let them rejoice at *my* downfall.

But [vav adversative!] I trust in *your* unfailing love. [*Hesed!*]

   I will rejoice because *you* have rescued me.

I will sing to the *Lord*

   because *he* has been so good to me. (NLT)

David has crossed the line from the fear of his enemy to trusting the unfailing love of his God. He has passed from complaint to worship. He has gone from the slavery of self-focus to the freedom of seeing only God. The *vav* marks a line in the center of the bridge of lament. Crossing the line is everything.

Lament is the means of crossing over from the anger of retributive justice to the mercy of *hesed*. If we are ever to move away from hating our enemies toward eventually loving them, as Jesus commands, we must first cross this bridge. We must submit to this process until God is finished with His process of perfecting our hearts. Until then, it is useless to stand in His presence and mouth pretended words of forgiveness and love.

I have a friend who says that revenge is "the poison we drink, hoping our enemy will die." The truth is, I have been drinking this poison all of my life, while the enemies I pretend I don't have grow stronger every day. The truth is, the One who commanded me to love those same enemies drank every drop of the poison that fills my heart and yours.

CHAPTER 13

DISEASE AND DEATH

"AS HE WENT, HE CRIED, 'O MY SON ABSALOM! MY SON, MY SON ABSALOM! If only I could have died instead of you — O Absalom, my son, my son!'" (2 Samuel 18:33, NIV). David lived long enough to endure the deaths of practically everyone he had ever loved. First it was his dearest friend, Jonathan, killed in a battle on Mount Gilboa along with his father Saul, who committed suicide. Both their bodies were cruelly crucified on a wall in Beth Shan. The valiant men of Jabesh Gilead journeyed through the night, stole back the bodies, burned and buried them. We are told in the first chapter of 2 Samuel that David composed a lament for the both of them; the man who most hated him and the friend he loved the most. David ordered that everyone in Judah learn the lament he had composed to a long-lost melody he entitled "The Song of the Bow."

"How the mighty have fallen!" David laments. Neither his bitterest enemy nor his dearest friend would return from this battle. He describes them both using words like, "beloved," "gracious." The both of them were "swifter than eagles" and "stronger than lions." But neither were swift nor strong enough to escape the deaths that awaited them on the desolate mountain of Gilboa. Through his tears, David pictures Jonathan lying dead upon the hills because he cannot bring himself to see him hanging crucified on the walls of Beth Shan.

"How I weep for you, my brother Jonathan," David sings to the strains of that long forgotten melody as he dissolves into tears (2 Samuel 1:26).

> "Evil and pain will not have the last word. The valley of the
> shadow of death is not our final destination."
> MICHAEL JINKINS[1]

A DISTURBING CLARITY

Next in the mournful procession was the innocent child born of his sin with Bathsheba. In the midst of the most successful period of his reign, having defeated the Ammonites and the Arameans, David took a suspicious break from what had been an almost continuous war. Even though it was spring, the time of year when kings normally returned to the battlefield, David stayed home, sending Joab out in his stead. But he learned that there are more wars to be fought in the spring than those of the battlefield.

Nine months later, a son was born whose name we will never know. Nathan told David the innocent child was going to die for his sin. Then we are told that the child, still referred to as being of "Uriah's wife," became ill (2 Samuel 12:15). Despite all David's pleading, despite his fasting and prayers, the nameless little boy died on the seventh day. (Had he lived but one more day, he would have been dedicated and so would have died with a name.)[2]

Everyone was afraid to tell David the bad news, so great had been his lamenting of the child's sickness. How would he respond? But when finally he heard of the little boy's death, David underwent an unusual and unexpected transformation. He got up off the ground. He took a bath and put on clean clothes. He went to worship. Finally, he went home to break his weeklong fast. His servants simply could not understand the sudden change in his emotional state.

David's response reveals the kind of disturbing clarity that only lament affords:

"While he was alive there was still a chance," he said. "I thought
to myself, 'Who knows, maybe the Lord will let the boy live. But
now he is gone and nothing I can do will bring him back. I will
someday go to be with him, but he will never return to me."
(2 Samuel 12:22-23, my paraphrase)

It is usually seen as merely the next event in the chronological chain, but the
connection between this event and the next is important. David laments the
loss of his baby son and then, having exhausted himself in lament, he returns
to comfort Bathsheba, now his wife. Out of that comfort, Solomon is born, the
boy God named Jedidiah, "beloved of the Lord." The same stubborn refusal to
let go of God that is expressed in his laments empowered David to stubbornly
refuse to be destroyed by the grief of innocent death and the despair of knowing it was all a consequence of his sin. The painful realities of death and sin had
somehow been "dealt with" during his time of lament. They had been offered
in worth-ship to the God David was beginning to learn could be trusted.

Lament leads us in the direction of that kind of clarity. Only by realizing
the reality of the pain and acknowledging through lament to God our pow-
erlessness and hopelessness, can we arrive at such a place of freedom as David
inhabited. Innocent children die as a result of the sins of others every second
on this planet. As much as we can bear, the pain needs to be acknowledged.
But on the other side, by God's grace, a comfort comes. On the other side of
the line that every lament must cross, *hesed* is always waiting. And by it, every
day more children are born who are "beloved by the Lord."

A Disturbing Despair

David's son, Absalom, was handsome. He was vain. It was said of him
that "he stole the hearts of the men of Israel." In a fit of righteous rage
he murdered his own brother, Amnon, for the rape of his sister Tamar. In
fear of reprisals, he ran away to his grandfather's and hid for three years.

When finally he slinked back to Jerusalem, David refused to speak to him for another two years. The rift between David and Absalom would never be healed. In time, he would lead a successful revolt, forcing his father David to flee Jerusalem. His name literally means "the father of peace." But it was precisely the peace of his father that Absalom obliterated by his pride.

When finally their two armies fought near the forests of Ephraim, Absalom lost twenty thousand of his own men. As he fled we are told his long hair got tangled in the boughs of a tree and he was slain.

David sat pitifully, waiting at the gate like the father of the prodigal who would never return. When finally he heard the news, in stark contrast to the miraculous recovery we just saw after the death of Bathsheba's first son, David broke down completely. For once, he did not compose a formal lament. "O my son Absalom! My son, my son Absalom! If only I had died instead of you — O Absalom, my son, my son!" (2 Samuel 18:33; 19:4, NIV). There was no tune. There was no poetry, only the repetitious, incoherent sobbing of a father whose son, though he had just died, he had lost long ago.

THE DIS-EASE OF ABANDONMENT

When faced with a lingering disease, David, apparently more than once, composed psalms of lament.

Psalm 6 is tagged as a *sheminith*, the Hebrew word for "eight." Some scholars believe this is a musical term denoting the lowest note that can be sung by a male voice. Others think it may be a reference to an eight-stringed instrument. In this lament David cries out to the Lord for healing. "How long?" he groans again and again, like an impatient patient. (In Psalm 13 he also repeatedly cries out, "How long?" but finds rest in the end in the trust he has in God's *hesed*.) He confesses his terror in verse 3 but still appeals to God on the basis of His *hesed* in the following verse. Though the presence of disease causes David to question the mysterious inconsistencies of God's *hesed*, he refuses to doubt neither the existence nor the reality of it. From our limited perspective, disease and death will always seem inconsistent with God's lov-ing-kindness. But, at the same time, the foundation of all the hope in every lament is always *hesed* as well.

The ever-present enemies that seem to always be lurking in the shadows of David's life reappear in all the disease laments. From his sickbed he calls out to them, "Away from me!" (Psalm 6:8, NIV). In this, as well as other laments of disease, there is a troubling awareness in the psalmist that his sickness, like Job's, might provide proof to his enemies that he is guilty of some unspoken sin. Through his lament he seeks God's forgiveness, healing, and protection from this shame in the presence of his enemies. Present also in the disease laments is a sense of being cut off from the community at large by this false indication of guilt.

Darkest of all David's sickness laments is Psalm 38. (Some might argue that Psalm 22 is the most despairing, but I do not read it simply as a psalm of disease. Its scope is far greater.) The language is full of the blackest sorts of imaginings and images. The sickness feels like arrows piercing his flesh. His wounds are festering and loathsome. There is a burning pain in his back. His heart is pounding. He seems to have become blind as well as deaf and mute. Perhaps even more painful is the rejection and abandonment of his friends and neighbors. The hurtful implication once more is that they keep their dis-tance because they believe his illness is the result of sin. Maybe they showed up at first, like Job's friends, to comfort him. But now they are all gone.

While his friends have vanished, his enemies seem to be everywhere. They gloat. They slander and hate him for no reason.

DEATH'S DARK CLOUD

It is clear that God redeemed David's personal, intimate experience of disease and death and used it to put words to the pain and suffering for all of us; for those who are suffering as well as those who long to better understand and enter into the suffering of others. David's laments of sickness tell us that even physical suffering is rooted in one dark and basic fear: being separated from the Presence of God. Deep inside us something knows that this separation would literally be "hell." Disease threatens us by its very existence, which tempts us to fear that God is separate, is not present, is hiding, is asleep, has forgotten. In David's mind, hell is the hidden face of God.

Death, by its dark finality, poses the final unknowable test of faith. All of us are left standing on this side of that threatening door with the fear that when we do pass through we might not find God waiting for us on the other side.

Author Albert Y. Hsu gives us this perspective on death and grief:

> Christians sometimes think that we are not supposed to grieve,
> because our faith and theology provide us with confidence about
> heaven and eternal life. But while 1 Thessalonians 4:13 says
> that we are not to grieve as those who have no hope, we grieve
> nevertheless. Those without hope grieve in one way; those with
> hope grieve in another. Either way, grief is universal and not to
> be avoided. It is a legitimate response to loss.[3]

The Fall that ushered lament into the world is a dark cloud, a cloud of unknowing. When death and disease come we are enveloped for a time in the cloud. As it blows over us, we fear it might cut us off from the healing, resurrecting Presence. For one confused moment we misunderstand, thinking its very existence is the ultimate contradiction to *hesed*. For one brief instant we cannot see the face of our Father. Through lament we push into and through (not around) the cloud. Only then do we completely reach the other side, the place where we find Jesus waiting for us.

If you think about it, there isn't much in life that isn't "life threatening." We all carry deep within ourselves a pressurized reservoir of tears. It takes only the right key at the right time to unlock them. The lock can be forced or the unlocking can happen prematurely, to our ruin. But in God's perfect time, through lament, when these tears are released, they can form a vast healing flood.

CHAPTER 14

NO HOPE BUT THIS: CONTRITION

AMIDST THE DEARTH OF OUR KNOWLEDGE OF THE PSALMS, IT IS THE SINGLE psalm of lament for which we all seem to know the historical background. In a life that had more than its share of ups and downs, it undeniably marks the lowest ebb in the life of David.

As we have already seen, it was spring and David had decided to stay at home instead of going out to war. His men, under the leadership of Joab, were laying siege to the Ammonite city of Rabbah.

It was one of those beautiful spring evenings that calls you from your bed and lures you outside under the stars. David had heard that call and was taking an evening walk on the roof of his palace.

She was taking a bath, washing away her "uncleanness," when David saw her beautiful form. While hers was merely ceremonial, David's uncleanness was shamelessly real and he immediately set about realizing it.

He quickly found out who she was, the wife of one of his faithful soldiers named Uriah. He was a Hittite, a descendant of a fierce tribe that once rivaled Egypt itself. Its rulers, the powerful Hyksos, had become pharaohs in Egypt for a time, the shepherd kings. The Egyptians described them as "yellow skinned." His wife was named Bathsheba.

There is no mention of any struggle, no reference to rape. But how was a woman supposed to say "no" to the king? After their single encounter, she became pregnant and sent word of it to David.

At once, David sent for Uriah, ordering him to go home in hopes of hiding the paternity of the baby. But the Hittite chose to sleep, not in the warm bed of his beautiful wife, but on the cold floor at the door of David's palace. When David later asked him why, Uriah responded with the kind of ancient dedication to war for which his people were famous. If his fellow soldiers were sleeping in a field, how could he bring himself to enjoy the comforts of home? In his simple, loyal heart, Uriah found the notion unthinkable. Even after David manipulated him into getting drunk, the Hittite would not give in to the temptation to return to Bathsheba.

Finally, with the collusion of Joab, David in effect murdered Uriah by placing him in the front of the battle lines, ordering his companions to fall back from him, leaving him to his fate. The plan worked with sickening perfection. Uriah, the descendant of so many fierce warriors, died treacherously, his yellow skin stained with his own red blood.

She seems a silent cipher in the story. Never do we hear a word from those beautiful lips. When Bathsheba learns of her husband's death she obediently mourns for him, though we do not know the depth of her sincerity. When her time of mourning is over, she moves into David's house and dutifully becomes his wife. Where else can she go? Soon the baby is born. "But the thing David had done," the Bible says, "displeased the Lord" (2 Samuel 11:27, NIV).

In 2 Samuel 12, Nathan appears. We are told in both the Chronicles that he later wrote a life of David.[1] If only those documents had survived, we might be able to read his own account of this sad story.

Nathan is a prophet which means by definition that he says what God would say in any given situation. Later, when God Incarnate would appear, His favorite form of teaching would be the parable that Nathan used.

The power of Nathan's parable disarms and draws David in. It engages his imagination, the door between his heart and mind. By its very form it begins the process of reintegrating the disintegrated king. Nathan uses the power of story to break David in the best sense of the word.

He launches into the parable without a word of explanation, so David doesn't know if it's fact or fiction. So gifted a storyteller is the prophet that David falsely concludes that it must be a true story. It is true only in the metaphorical sense, though the story itself is fiction. The truth of it is deeper and truer than simple historical fact. The fiction of it tells the fact of David's abomination:

> "There were two men, one rich the other poor," began Nathan. "The man who was rich had herds of sheep and cattle. The poor man possessed only a single lamb. But to him it was not a possession but rather a pet. It drank from his cup and slept in his arms.
>
> "A hungry traveler showed up on the rich man's door step, but the rich man, instead of using one of his own sheep or cattle decided to slaughter the poor man's pet lamb" (my paraphrase).

Every good parable lacks closure, and Nathan's is no exception. He leaves the story just there, no moralizing, no conclusion, because of course he wants David to make the conclusion on his own. Which he does.

As his imagination becomes fully engaged, David's indignation erupts. "He should die for such a thing," he shouts, "but before he goes to the gallows, he must pay four times the value because he showed no pity!"

Just then, their eyes met across the throne room, Nathan's knowing gaze with David's ignorant, angry glare. There was a moment of silence and in that moment, just before Nathan opened his mouth, David sensed deep in his spirit that something was about to go terribly wrong, something far worse than Nathan's story.

"You are the man!" He violates the strict protocol of the court and points a boney finger at David. "Why did you despise the Lord by doing this evil thing?"

As Nathan continues the divine invective, David, looking down at the polished marble floor can only mutter, "I have sinned against the Lord."

God had graciously given David everything a man could ever imagine wanting. But David wanted more, no matter what pain it might cost Uriah or Bathsheba or even God. The small scale of the make-believe sin of Nathan's parable that had so enraged the king looms large now. David was angered over the loss of a lamb. Now he is utterly broken in the revelation that the life of a noble and courageous man, created in the image of God, has been treacherously murdered. A kingdom has been thrown away for a moment's passion. The story begins to sound like a King Arthur tale once more.

Psalm 51 was written in the throes of David's sorrowful repentance. There is an immediacy in its mournful tone that would not be there if he had waited very long to "compose" a proper lament. This is not a king confessing; it is a completely broken man crying out to the God he knows is his last hope.

"Have mercy on me, O God," laments David, "according to your [*hesed*]" (Psalm 51:1, NIV). *Hesed* is his only hope, and so David clings to the hope of it like a man clinging to a piece of driftwood in the midst of a storm. It is not the deserved retributive justice he had so angrily called down on the rich man in Nathan's parable that David wants, it is undeserved grace and mercy that he now knows he cannot live without. For now he knows he will never deserve it. Only undeserved grace will blot out his transgressions. Only the clean waters of *hesed* could possibly wash away all of this foul iniquity and sin from his life.

Though it cost Bathsheba her marriage and Uriah his life, David writhes in knowing that, in the end, all sin is sin against God. "Against you, you only, have I sinned," he cries. The single One he offended is also his only hope. His Judge must also be his Savior. If his life is ever to be made right once more, David knows now it is not in his power to do it. The purity he might have thought was his own accomplishment is a fantasy. He utters eight simple words that will be echoed by countless others after him. David puts to words the hopeless cry of all our hearts:

"Create in me a pure heart, O God" (Psalm 51:10, NIV).

In his despair, David pleads for God to refrain from doing something even His vast omnipotence would find impossible to do. "Do not cast me from your presence or take your Holy Spirit from me" (verse 11).

Does David still not understand that sharing His presence with his servant David had been God's deepest desire all along? That's why He had called David out of the obscurity of Bethlehem and crowned him king. That's why He placed in David's heart the desire to renew the worship of the Tabernacle of God.[2] That's why He had been present with him through all those deadly battles, when "thousands fall at his side." That's why God had saved David, so he would not be cast from His presence. Were it not for the grace of His *hesed*, David's sin *would* have cast him from God's presence.

David can think of only one more request. If God will grant him a willing spirit to sustain him, the joy of his salvation will be restored. The hope of the reappearance of any semblance of joy in his shattered life must have come to David from outside himself. Who but God could have possibly granted for it to even be imagined, much less asked for?

From now on, it is all about the promises of what David will do in response:

He will teach . . .

He will sing . . .

He will declare . . .

In a moment of illumination, David finally sees that all he has left to give is all that God wants from him. Before Bathsheba, David might have offered his fame, his many victories, his wealth, or any one of a thousand other of his "strengths." All he has left is all God wants, his spirit that is broken and his heart that is contrite. He knows now, as he could have never known otherwise, that God accepts him, unclean and hopeless. The knowledge of this sets David and each of us forever free.

(Put down this book now and pick up the Psalms. In this order, read these laments of David: 27; 22; 13; 38; 51; 55; 109; and 69. This will probably take a little more than an

hour. When you are finished, give yourself some quiet time with the Lord, not seeking to understand these laments but more in an effort to "enter into" them. Allow their sorrow, frustration, confusion, and hate to mingle with your own. Finally, after a good span of thoughtful time, read Psalms 32; 8; 103; and 23.

A Lament: "Crossing the Bridge"

Lord, between You and me lies a deep chasm,
> The dark gorge of my doubt,
I cannot see a way across to Light, to Hope, to You
Jesus, between us an impossible valley of shadows is fixed
And if I enter in, will I not die?

Stranded, hopeless, I call out, breathlessly across the void.
With words,
> empty words,
> > the clumsy bricks of words
I hurl across my fears, my hatreds, my last shredded hopes
They are all I have left,
They are all that You want.

Here I hopelessly stand, I can do no other.
It is to You to find me, or I will never be found.
I wait then, in the shadows, a sheep, Your sheep.
Lost, lost, hopelessly lost.

If You be Shepherd, come, find, mend, protect, save
And on Your shoulders carry me to verdant pasture and living water

PART FOUR

***

JEREMIAH

CHAPTER 15

A DIFFICULT HOPE

WE KNOW MORE ABOUT JEREMIAH THAN ANY OTHER OLD TESTAMENT prophet, yet we're not even sure what his name means. The scholars' best guess is something like, "the Lord casts down." But even this translation, no one is willing to bet on.

"Cast down" . . . it seems to capture Jeremiah's life in a nutshell. Born in the poverty-stricken village of Anathoth, in the sad territory of Benjamin, a forever impoverished part of the country, all desert and deserted, the way his life would turn out.

He was most likely a descendant of Abiathar, the treacherous priest who, in collusion with Adonijah, sought to rob Solomon of his throne. Because of his betrayal he was cursed and though they were a priestly family, none of Jeremiah's kin were ever permitted to minister in the newly restored "ark shrine" of David (1 Kings 2:26). And so Jeremiah grew up in a barren place, among men who were denied their priestly purpose in life.

Due to the "last days" character of his times, the Lord commanded him not to marry (Jeremiah 16:1-4), which is enough to make anyone feel "cast down."[1] And so there entered into the barren landscape of his life this additional desolation. If Jeremiah could not find it in himself to make the Lord his one true Companion in life, he would be forced to wander through the lonely wilderness of his life completely alone.

Regardless of what his name might mean, or might have meant to him,

Jeremiah apparently never gave in to its dismal prophetic ring. I imagine him as a boy, every time he heard himself being called by that name, whispering inside himself, "Cast down maybe, but never broken!"

Jeremiah was somehow able to weather the repeated desert storms of his life and times and still remain upright. His own people turned against him. The majority of the five kings to whom he sought to minister the "word of the Lord" rejected him as well. Only the first king, Josiah, seems to have appreciated the prophet at all.

When Josiah is murdered, Jeremiah laments (2 Chronicles 35:25). Had he known what the next king, Jehoahaz, would be like, his lament surely would have been even longer. Jehoahaz fell into idolatry (2 Kings 23:32) and was deposed by Pharaoh-Necho, taken captive into Egypt, where he eventually died.[2]

In one of the most twisted scenes in the Old Testament, Jehoiakim, warming himself by a winter fire in his palace, takes a pen knife and cruelly cuts the scroll containing Jeremiah's prophecies into small pieces, throwing them, one by one, into the flames (Jeremiah 36:20-32). This would have been enough to cause anyone to lose hope, but not Jeremiah. At the Lord's command, he started all over again, producing a new scroll with the aid of his scribe, Baruch, the only real friend he ever had.[3] The final chapter of his great prophecy seems to have been added by the faithful hand of Baruch.

From Jeremiah's point of view it could be said that even God eventually abandoned him. But by the end of his life, standing amidst the rubble of Jerusalem as well as the wreckage of his own existence, Jeremiah had *survived*. How he was able to do this is one of the most important questions we can ask of his lamentable life. If David is the ultimate composer and Job our mentor of lament, Jeremiah is the penultimate example for the incarnation of lament, of lament in-fleshed and lived out. How he so steadfastly held on to such a difficult hope is a story worth telling.

CHAPTER 16

DARK, FAMILIAR ECHOES

JEREMIAH'S WORLD AND LIFE SITUATION ARE STRIKINGLY SIMILAR TO THOSE of Job and David, our other two "lamenters." The times were unstable both politically and theologically for Israel. After the glorious reforms of Josiah (640-609 BC), the political world of Jeremiah and his people slid back into one dominated by the power and greed of kings like Jehoahaz (609 BC) and Jehoiachin (598-597 BC). Zedekiah, perhaps the most ruthless of them all, imprisoned Jeremiah. This confusing, decades-long shepherd-less existence sounds much like the stage onto which the young David, our psalmist of lament, first stepped. For both Jeremiah and David, it became painfully clear early in life that if hope were ever to be found, it would not be in the world of men.

In the larger, global scene, Jeremiah was forced to live the uncertain existence forced on those who are caught up between the world's great powers. This is the hopeless position so well known by those who struggle in what we refer to today as the "third world." In Jeremiah's time the ongoing and endless conflicts were between three powerful rulers: Ashurbanipal, the last great ruler of Assyria; Nabopolassar, who created the Neo-Babylonian empire; and the Pharaoh of Egypt, Necho II. Israel would always manage to find herself somewhere in the middle of their larger conflicts. As Jeremiah sought to advise the different kings of Israel, of whom only Josiah ever listened, he was forced into the inescapable dilemma of the prophet, which was so well worded by Elie Wiesel: Only if the prophet tells the truth can the prophecy prove to be false.[1] That is, if somehow Jeremiah had been able to convince the kings to listen to the Lord, then inevitably the destruction he had prophetically promised would have been averted. If the king bows to what the Lord wants and the people repent, then the prophecy is canceled and no one will ever really know if it might have been true.

Our friend Job was no stranger to this kind of unstable world. His own sufferings began when the second millennium warring tribes of the Sabeans and the Chaldeans descended on his lands and destroyed everything (Job 1:15,17). He understood the hopelessness of being the pawn, forever caught in the middle. Again, we must remind ourselves of our original question: Just how was Jeremiah able to survive such a lamentable world? Did he survive it in the same way Job and David survived?

The conflicts of the theological life situation of Jeremiah echo that of both David and Job, but more particularly, Job. A subtle shift was occurring between two theological world views: one dominated by a narrow rationale of retributive justice, the other by the mystery of *hesed*. The strains of this struggle are clearly seen in the writings of one of Jeremiah's contemporaries, Habakkuk.

His little book, which is often referred to as the "Job of the Prophets," wrestles with precisely the same issue — the conflict between retributive justice and *hesed*. The book, which bears little resemblance to any of the other Prophets, contains a dialogue of lament between Habakkuk and God. What separates it from the book and the experience of Job is that in Habakkuk, God actually offers up answers!

In God's first response (Habukkuk 1:5-11), He hints at an unbelievable new world of *hesed* with which He will someday flood the world: "For I am going to do something in your days that you would not believe, even if you were told" (1:5, NIV).

God proceeds to describe for Habakkuk the same unthinkable destruction of Jerusalem by the Babylonians that Jeremiah was also forced to prophetically see and eventually tragically experience.

Habakkuk concludes with a psalm that echoes David's formulas of remembrance (3:3-7) as well as Job's words concerning the awesomeness of God over creation (3:8-12). In two significant phrases, he speaks of the fact that the lines between the grace that comes by faith, and mercy and justice, will be crossed someday, at least in Habakkuk's mind and heart:

"The just shall live by his faith." (2:4, KJV)

"In wrath remember mercy." (3:2, KJV)

Amidst these dark echoes of political and theological confusion, squeezed in the vicious vise of a leaderless country and a threatening world, Habakkuk sings a truth that both David and Job sang before him, a truth that somewhere else in the land of Israel, Jeremiah was only beginning to learn to sing. That is, the God of Israel, who is the God of the universe, remembers, acts, and responds according to a "surprising mercy," an "unexpected forgiveness." He is determined, whatever the cost, to be known by His *hesed*. As He looks down on His frustrated, inconsistently Torah-abiding children, He says in effect, "How could you ever think that that was only all I was?"

Those who would hold on long enough to sing this unimaginable, new song, those like Job, David, Habakkuk, and Jeremiah, kept their grip by not letting go of God through the painful means of honest lament.

CHAPTER 17

TORN BETWEEN TWO LOVES

AS WE HAVE SEEN, JEREMIAH WAS A PRIEST (JEREMIAH 1:1), WHICH MEANS HE was supposed to know what it felt like to stand before God and offer a sacrifice for the sins of the people. But he was also called to be a prophet, albeit a reluctant one (Jeremiah 1:6). And a prophet is called to offer to the people, in effect, the sacrificial, sacramental Words of God. Rarely was any man called to both of these desperate offices. Only, some four hundred years later, would Someone perfectly fulfill both offices by being the Word who was sacrificed for the people.[1]

These two great and conflicting roles struggled to come together in Jeremiah. But even after the disastrous destruction of Jerusalem had occurred, he must have found it difficult to grasp that, as priest, he had witnessed the people destroyed by their own sin. And that, as prophet, he had spoken the Word of God to ears that would never hear. Out of this frustration his laments would flow as Jeremiah found himself torn between his deep love for his own people, Israel, and his intense, personal, fearful affection for God.

In one of his first oracles, Jeremiah announced to Israel that God could no longer bear with her faithlessness (2-3). What is most striking about this prophecy from the very mind and mouth of God is that it sounds remarkably like a lament. God is lamenting through Jeremiah to His people:

"What fault did your fathers find in me, that they strayed so far from me?"(2:5, NIV).

"They have forsaken me, the spring of living water" (2:13, NIV).

And perhaps most heart-breaking of all: "I thought you would call me 'Father' and not turn away from following me" (3:19, NIV).

God's own heart had been broken by His unfaithful people. The One whom Jeremiah discovered was moved by his tears was now weeping for Himself, lamenting the loss of His beloved. Jeremiah, who would weep so many tears on behalf of his people, wept first the tears of his betrayed God. His lament is the only bridge that seems to have survived the destruction. It is a surprising place to find oneself in, reaching out to a God who is moved by our tears and who, more often than we could imagine, weeps His own tears through us.

Jeremiah's tears flow from God's anger as well as His pain. Though Jeremiah had himself felt the pain of their rejection, it is the prophet's identification with God's indignation that gives birth to his bitterest complaints. In his first great complaint (12:1-4), to which God gives answer in verses 5-17, Jeremiah says to God, about the people: "You are always on their lips, but far from their hearts" (12:2, NIV).

Before he proceeds to his next imprecation, Jeremiah makes the careful preliminary statement, "You know me, O Lord. You see me and test my thoughts about You," lest God fail to recognize that Jeremiah has not lost sight of the dangerous dimensions of his own anger. Next erupts a surprising and venomous statement that only hints at the inner turmoil and pain with which the conflicted prophet will struggle for the rest of his life. To experience the depths of the emotional life of God, to weep His tears and give voice to His pain: how could any human bear such a burden? Of his own beloved people, Jeremiah screams,

"Drag them off like sheep to be butchered!

Set them apart for the day of slaughter!" (verse 3, NIV).

In a later complaint passage (20:7-18), Jeremiah vents his anger and frustration in the other direction, toward God Himself! After Pashhur, the son of the chief priest in the temple, had Jeremiah beaten and placed in the stocks, the prophet turns around and attacks God:

O Lord, you deceived me, and I
    was deceived;
you overpowered me and prevailed.
I am ridiculed all day long;
    everyone mocks me.
Whenever I speak, I cry out
    proclaiming violence and destruction.
So the word of the Lord has brought me
    insult and reproach all day long.
But if I say, "I will not mention him
    or speak any more in his name,"
his word is in my heart like a fire,
    a fire shut up in my bones.
I am weary of holding it in;
    indeed, I cannot. (NIV)

Caught between the obstinate disbelief of the people who refuse to listen to the Word of God that burns in his bones, and the almighty outrage and consuming bitterness of the betrayed Bridegroom, Jeremiah finally exhausts himself against God. Somehow internally, he mystically steps across a line. It is the same line we have seen Job and David cross so many times in their laments. Having emptied himself of himself, Jeremiah overflows in praise.

    Sing to the Lord!
    Give praise to the Lord!
    He rescues the life of the needy
    from the hands of the wicked. (verse 13)

Then, as inexplicably, perhaps his eyes having focused on the bruises on his wrists caused by the stocks, the tormented Jeremiah spits out an imprecation on himself. It could well be Job speaking:

Cursed be the day I was born!

    May the day my mother bore me not be blessed!

Cursed be the man who brought my father the news,

    who made him very glad, saying,

      "A child is born to you — a son!"

May that man be like the towns

    the Lord overthrew without pity.

May he hear wailing in the morning,

    a battle cry at noon.

For he did not kill me in the womb,

    with my mother as my grave,

    her womb enlarged forever.

Why did I ever come out of the womb

    to see trouble and sorrow

    and to end my days in shame? (verses 14-18, NIV)

    In the twists and turns of his life as a prophet of God and a priest for God, Jeremiah comes often to the end of his rope. Each time he discovers himself hanging there, he will find the strength to hold on (even as Job and David did) only by means of the honest laments that kept him connected to his difficult God in the service of His impossible people. In the truest place inside his heart, he loves them both so deeply. He longs to reconcile the two. His heart aches, like the friend of the bridegroom, to usher Israel the bride into the wedding feast to which God had invited her again and again. The Bridegroom refuses to give up, motivated by His inexhaustible and inexplicable *hesed*. The bride stubbornly, blindly, deafly, refuses to give in. Jeremiah stands between the two with a hand resting on them both (recall Job.9:33), called to reconcile the irreconcilable. Impossibly ill-equipped, outrageously inadequate to the task that would only eventually be perfectly carried out four hundred years in the future by the impoverished Prophet/Priest from Nazareth. Jesus would be the One who would eventually intercede by "laying a hand on them both, as

His hands were outstretched on a cross."

I find it striking that at least once, Jesus was mistaken for Jeremiah (Matthew 16:14). Perhaps it was the tears that often coursed down His cheeks. Perhaps it was His own prophecies of the coming destruction of Jerusalem (Luke 19:41; Matthew 27:37). Jesus would use Jeremiah's words to describe His own anger and pain (Matthew 21:13). Jesus would, after all, finally bridge the gap, the vise, in which Jeremiah had been caught and eventually crushed. Jesus, the priest, would offer at last a perfect sacrifice before God on behalf of the people. The perfect Prophet, Jesus, would speak the lament on behalf of the God who had been forsaken once again by His people in those darkest words of David, "Why have You forsaken me?" Jeremiah had been torn between the people and God. Jesus would be torn apart by them.

CHAPTER 18

LAMENTATIONS: THE DESTRUCTION OF JEREMIAH

✤

TO THE WEST OF JERUSALEM THERE LIES A ROCKY HILL, JUST OUTSIDE THE Damascus gate. In the face of that hill is a cave that from ancient times was called the "grotto of Jeremiah." It is said that after Nebuchadnezzar's annihilation of the holy city, Jeremiah fled there to write his lamentations. The sound of weeping that echoed from that cave made it clear that the destruction of Jerusalem had destroyed Jeremiah too.

It seems remarkable that the longest book of the Bible, Jeremiah, should provide the introduction for one of the shortest, Lamentations. Standing just behind him, in the cave that overlooked the ruined city, we must read Lamentations as if we were looking over Jeremiah's shoulder as he wrote. The smoldering desolation of the once beautiful city might eerily remind us of the smoking ruins of the World Trade Towers. For many in our time, it was as equally unimaginable as the event that first called forth Jeremiah's laments. Perhaps we might even hope Jeremiah will give us words to voice the outrage and shock in our own world that he lamented in his. Perhaps in his writings we might begin to understand the consequences of our own sin.

We would expect a certain gut-wrenching, frantic disorganization from Jeremiah's Lamentations. In fact, we find an amazing degree of literary structure. The book is composed of four acrostic poems (like the Davidic laments of Psalms 25, 34, and 37). Each verse begins with a letter of the Hebrew alphabet. This literary form serves two important practical functions. First, it provides a mnemonic device for the congregation of Israel which still reads Lamentations every year on the ninth of Ab, the day of mourning for the destruction of the Temple. Secondly, the alphabetic structure is used to teach small children the alphabet.

Seen over Jeremiah's shoulder, the book opens with a series of portraits of the city as a lonely widow, weeping the loss of her beloved. She is the queen who has become a slave. She is the virgin daughter whose eyes now overflow with tears because she has been rejected and can find no one to comfort her. It is as if Jeremiah must force himself to keep finding examples to say what it is *like* in order to save himself the torture of having to put into words what it actually *is*.

In the second poem of lament, the absent Groom of chapter one is transformed into an angry, pitiless enemy who has "hurled down the splendor" and covered Zion with "the cloud of his anger." To the inconceivable image of a destroyed Jerusalem, Jeremiah adds the unimaginable notion that the Lord God of Israel has become their enemy, that the once protective cloud of His presence has become a storm cloud. He has "overthrown you without pity," laments the weeping prophet. All those things that seemed to matter most to the Lord — His Sanctuary, His feasts, His altar — He has Himself destroyed. As the terrifying notion occurs to Jeremiah that God had, in fact, planned all this long ago, he runs out of words. "What can I say to you?" he sobs. All that is left for the terrified survivors is to "cry out in the night," "pour out your heart like water," and "let your tears flow like a river." Jeremiah asks the rhetorical question, "Whom have you ever treated like this?" The moaning of the wind that whips past the entrance of the cave blends with the distant wailing of the forsaken widows of Jerusalem. The only answer to his desolate question is the forsaken silence.

In chapter 3 (NIV), the tone of Lamentations shifts once more as Jeremiah steps from behind the curtain of all his metaphors and speaks first person. "*I* am the man who has seen affliction!" he laments. "He has driven *me* away!" He has turned his hand against *me*!" "He has besieged *me,* surrounded *me,* weighed *me,* walled in *me*!" In return for his faithfulness, Jeremiah has become a "laughingstock." They have made up songs to mock him. Any fleeting and fragmented peace, prosperity, or splendor he might have ever known has vanished in the rubble of the ruined city.

And then mysteriously, miraculously the turn happens. In verse 22, the mystical line of the Hebrew letter *vav* is crossed. Jeremiah has exhausted himself against the God who has become his enemy. Having poured all of himself out in lament, he finds in his hopeless emptiness a greater hope than he could have imagined: the surprising hope of *hesed.*

"Because of the Lord's great *hesed* we are not consumed."

All that stands between him and the nothingness of being forgotten by God is *hesed.* "His compassions never fail," he sings, and one wonders if there is any possibility that he is singing about the same God in chapter 3 that was the source of all his sorrows in chapters 1 and 2. The "compassion" of the God of the first two chapters had obviously failed long ago. Just look around at the ruins. But now, in its place, Jeremiah overflows in the kind of praise that only pours from lament. To be sure, it is a bruised and bloody praise. It will always bear the same sort of limp that Jacob endured after he wrestled and exhausted himself against God that dark night by the ford of the Jabbok (Genesis 32:22). But it is a praise that can now hope all things, having been forced to let go of everything. It is a praise that rushes in to fill utterly every crack and corner of Jeremiah's emptied soul. It is not a praise whose source is human feelings or emotions. After all, they are exhausted, virtually nonexistent by now. No, this is praise that comes out of nowhere and everywhere. It comes from far beyond and yet from deep within at the same illuminating moment. We saw it when Job collapsed amidst the ruins of his life. We heard it when David cried out from the wilderness of his own hopelessness. Once tasted, this praise leaves every other pretended praise tasteless. It issues forth from the rubble of a once holy city. It can only come from the fragmented ruins of a once whole life. It can only echo from the wilderness.

"It is good," continues Jeremiah, "to wait quietly for Him," "to hope in Him," "to seek Him." A man may be left alone in silence, may have to bury his face in the dust or offer his cheek to one who would strike him, but, promises Jeremiah through his tears, "men are not cast off by the Lord forever." And why? Because so great is His *hesed*.

Notice how realistic Jeremiah's perspective has become. It contains a reality that didn't exist before. He allows for more suffering in the future, more slaps in the face, more moments of unbearable aloneness. The chapter concludes with more images of the God who "covers Himself in anger." But Jeremiah also has the assurance of the God who "looks down from heaven and sees." And what does He see? He sees the tears that have flowed in unceasing streams from the prophet's tired eyes. Jeremiah wept and God saw. He cried and God heard. He is not the God who waves the magic wand and makes the Babylonians or the cancer go away. He is the God who sees and hears and enters into the suffering *with* His suffering people in the wilderness. This God, Jeremiah could have never known in the marble palaces of Jerusalem, only from the windy cave that now overlooks the ruined city.

Jeremiah steps back behind the curtain in chapter 4. His tears seem to have dried for the moment. His eyes have cleared as well and with a piercing gaze he compares the present desolation with the glory that once was.

"The gold has lost its luster." (4:1)
"The former whiteness of the princes is now covered in soot." (4:7)

With an eery calm he coldly calculates that it is better to die by the sword than by famine. The siege of Jerusalem had lasted for two long years. During that time Jeremiah witnessed the hopeless horrors of famine that continue today in places like Sudan, amidst our otherwise prosperous, well-fed world. Maintaining his chilling objectivity, Jeremiah utters the most disturbing sentence in all the Bible. "The hands of compassionate women boiled their own children." In a book like Lamentations that focuses so much on the suffering and mourning of women, Jeremiah gives a voice to those who usually remain voiceless in history: the victims. It is usually the victors, after all, who write the story. But this unthinkable aspect of their suffering will never be forgotten, as indeed it never should, lest more women and children continue to suffer in such horrific ways.

The final chapter is an extended plea that the Lord "remember." What follows is a detailed list of what Jeremiah hopes the Lord will not forget: they are now orphans; they are weary; they are bearing the punishment for their father's sins; their women have been ravished; their princes crucified ("hung up by their hands"). All joy is gone. All dancing has turned into mourning. The rubble still smolders. The starving children still wail in the night. "Remember, O Lord." Because Your remembering will somehow make things right in the end and we will be restored.

Shouldn't Jeremiah's demand to remember ring in our own ears? Lest we forget the smell of smoke and death. Lest we allow ourselves to forget the sounds of weeping and wailing, especially of the "daughters of Jerusalem" for whom Jeremiah spent so much of his concern and grief. As you stand behind Jeremiah, looking out over the rubble of the Temple, see if you don't also recognize some of the twisted girders of the World Trade Center. After all, both catastrophes struck cultures who thought themselves invulnerable. The laments of the tenderhearted poet-prophet might just provide some of us a new understanding, perhaps even a new vocabulary to voice our confusion and grief over what is going on in our world. It might even call us to the place of repentance, a place to which Jeremiah's pathetic pleas were at last able to bring his first listeners.

In the Hebrew Bible, Lamentations is simply titled *ekah*, or "how." That one small word contains the wrestling "unimaginability" of the book. It could not have been called "Why?" because from the first, that question is answered. Why did the city fall? Because of the refusal of God's people to hear the words Jeremiah had been pleading for almost forty years. Because of their unwillingness to recognize and repent of their sin. The tragedy he had spoken of so many times, and perhaps even seen in his various visions, seems to have been as unthinkable and heartbreaking to Jeremiah as to everyone else when it finally did occur. Because of Jeremiah's faithful preaching, none of the survivors seem to have been asking "why?" — only "how?"

Lamentations ends with a whimper rather than a bang. It is like the last flickerings of a candle just before its flame sinks into the wax. "Restore us to yourself, O LORD, that we may return; . . . unless You have utterly rejected us and are angry with us beyond measure."

The candle flamed up only a few times amidst the otherwise shadowy laments. At the end it seems about to be extinguished, like Jeremiah's hope. There still exists in his heart the hope of *hesed*. We heard him sing of it in chapter 3. The one who looks down, along with us, from the cave, exhausted, bleary-eyed, is no finished product in the end. He is, along with you and me, submitted to a process of coming to know this remarkable God who is moved by our tears, who even weeps along with us. This God is not the enemy Jeremiah accused Him at first of being, and the prophet knows it — for now anyway. By handing over Jerusalem to the enemy, God, who is so ruthlessly committed to incarnating the truth, was only making visible the truth that had been concealed for so long: Jerusalem had lost her true glory long before Nebuchadnezzar showed up outside her walls. The desolation of the Temple had slowly happened over the centuries as both priests and people became satisfied with offering only their prescribed sacrifices and no longer themselves. When personal sin was at first tolerated, then overlooked, and finally woven into a way of life. The true destruction of the Temple came at precisely the point when it became more a club for the religious elite and less the house of prayer for the poor that God had set it aside to be. By handing the city over to the Babylonians, God was only actualizing, making visible, "infleshing," what was already true. Now its barrenness was painfully plain to see. In the end, God was neither their enemy nor their judge, because, in handing them over, He had only pronounced the sentence they had passed upon themselves long before.

Even as God had earlier provided His servant David to give voice to the lament of his people, now He provides Jeremiah to speak the unspeakable destruction of God's City. Like Job, Jeremiah and his people had lost everything a person can lose: possessions, homes, families, even their homeland. Like Job, all they had left now was all they ever needed, and all God wanted for them: God present among them. Immanuel.

Having read through the chapter on Jeremiah, now put this book down and read Lamentations. It is a short book, taking only about twenty minutes to read through. Given its length, try meditating through it using an ancient form called the lectio divina *or "divine reading." This is a simple method that involves reading through a passage of Scripture three times. The first time, called the* lectio, *you simply let the words wash over you, never straining to "solve the puzzle." Initially you listen to the words of Scripture with the "ears of your heart." When you are finished with this first reading, spend some quiet time listening to what you remember about the text. This is called the "meditatio" or meditation.*

The second time, as you read, ask the Holy Spirit to speak directly to your heart through some phrase or word in the text. This is called the oratio. *Then spend some time savoring this word as a precious gift. Again, do not strain to decipher it, only receive it as a gift.*

On your final read through, move slowly once more through the entire book. When you come to the special verse that was the Spirit's gift to you, pause one final moment and listen to it with a heart of thanksgiving. Allow yourself to rest in the given-ness of God's Word to you. This is called the contemplatio.

This ancient method of reading the Bible is more about connecting with God and less about straining to achieve a didactic understanding of the text. It relies on the simple belief that, alone with the Scripture before God, anyone who is willing to come can receive the Word as a priceless gift.

A Lament: "You didn't fix me, You joined me!"

I acknowledge before You, Lord, the glaring gap in the difference between what I feel and what I believe.

Right now, I feel like You don't really care. So many situations in my life are out of control. Why don't You just fix them?

So much in and around me hurts right now. Why don't You just heal them?

Were I willing to take more time to pray, I'm feeling right now that from my side of things, this could become a shouting business. DO SOMETHING!

But, You have already done something, haven't You?

You did what it took to become familiar with all the sorrows that I feel pressing in on me even this very moment. You felt the gap between what You felt and what You believed, didn't You?

Jesus, I'm so sorry I said You didn't care. Is there anything I could say that would have caused You more pain than that?

You didn't come to fix things for me, did You? You came to join me. Thank You.

Can I ask You one more thing?

Would You, in the sacrament of this moment, enter right now into the holy of holies that is my hurt? Come in, not to fix but to simply be present. Be Immanuel inside that sacred, hurting place, even if it's for only a few precious moments.

I can feel You now inside me Lord, Jesus.

I'm so sorry.

Thank You.

PART FIVE

✤✤✤

JESUS

CHAPTER 19

TRUTH HELD TOGETHER

PAUL SAID, IN COLOSSIANS 1:17, THAT IN JESUS "ALL THINGS HOLD TOGETHER" (NIV). Not the least among the "all" that He is referring to is the *truth* of all things. Everything that is true comes together in the life of Jesus of Nazareth, who called Himself the Truth. That is, something that is true here and something else that is true in a far-off place, come together over distant cultures, denominations, and even times, only in Jesus of Nazareth. It is one of the central implications of the perfection of His life.

All the various truths we've seen, scattered throughout the Old Testament, over centuries of time, through the lives of men like Job, David, and Jeremiah, come together and find meaningful unity (they "hold together") only in Jesus Christ. In Him all these various truths become True.

When we focus more narrowly on what is true about lament, we will see that Jesus not only holds all these truths together in perfect unity, but that as they come together in Him they find a new illumination. As He incarnates them, as He literally fleshes them out, we are able to understand them in the new Light that is His life. They form a more meaningful whole. Let us walk back through the different lives of lament we've investigated and see, in a small way, how Jesus holds the truth of them all together.

THE COMING TOGETHER OF JOB'S CRISIS

We saw that Job's struggle began before the throne of God, when Satan appeared as his accuser. The force of the accusation was that Job had only been faithful because God had blessed him. If God would only remove His hand and allow suffering to enter Job's life, Satan hissed, the feeble fabric of the faith of the old man would be made clear, and Job would "let go" of God. Satan longed to prove the point that, for Job, the old equation was all that mattered. That his faithfulness was being bought by God's blessing.

Unaware of the heavenly debate of which he himself was the object, Job faced the mountain of pain Satan heaped upon his life. He bore it as best he could, holding on to the God he thought he knew by means of lament. Despite the shrill advice of his wife to curse God and end it all, despite the persistent theological nagging of his friends, Job refused to "leave the dance floor." Because of his suffering he foresaw the many missing symbols and ciphers of the incomplete equation. His vision of the coming Advocate/Redeemer could not have been arrived at by any other means than lament. In the end, Job remained faithful.

A thousand years later, the cosmic struggle we witnessed in the throne room scenes in the book of Job came together once and for all. Jesus, bloodied long before anyone laid a hand on Him, struggled in the Garden to reconcile His will with the Father's. He had lived a life of perfect obedience. Now, as the burden of the most costly act of submission ever required of any man bore down upon Him, as He looked at the infinite demand of the cross, would His obedience remain perfect? Would He remain faithful? Or would He "let go" of God and "leave the dance floor" before the music was over? Could Satan tempt Him to relapse back into the simplicity of the ancient equation? After all, the Deceiver might say, Jesus had been good, perfectly good. So shouldn't God bless Him for it? How could His Father require Jesus to drink the crushing cup of suffering for the world's sin? Jesus wasn't due suffering, but blessing.

Could it not have been a repeat of the same throne room scene we saw in Job? Only now, every dimension of what was true became incarnate in Jesus' experience. In Him all that was true about obedience, suffering, and salvation would hold together, though all of Satan's dark power sought to tear them apart. Was the Accuser snarling that Jesus had only lived the perfect life He lived because something was in it for Him? Now the time had come to make the exchange Job had made, only on an infinitely larger scale; to give up everything in order that we might receive everything.

In Jesus, it all held together. He remained faithful. He never let go. In the end of that ancient story, the joy came when Job got God back. In the end of the New Testament, the joy came when God got Jesus back. In the end of Job, God would command Job's friends to ask Job to pray for them. Job's faithfulness placed him in the role of advocate before God. Because of the faithful obedience of Jesus, now we pray to Him as Advocate, asking God for forgiveness.

THE VOICE OF DAVID'S LAMENTS

Without the life of Jesus, many of the details of David's laments would be otherwise unintelligible. The miracle is seen in the minutia. The macrocosm of throne room scenes and cosmic struggles is one thing, but the remarkable coming together of the ordinary, small-scale objects like dice, seamless coats, and vinegar-soaked sponges speak from the other side of the scale of how perfectly Jesus' life "held together."

Few people realize that David's laments contain a more detailed description of the crucifixion than any of the Gospels. Psalm 69:21 speaks of the vinegar Jesus was given to drink. Psalm 109:25 tells of the mocking of the crowd. Psalm 22:18 predicts the soldiers gambling for Jesus' coat. But Psalm 22:16 contains the real treasure. It alone provides the painful detail given nowhere in the gospel account: "They have pierced my hands and feet."

Look as long as you like at Matthew, Mark, Luke, or John and you will not find this detail. For the most part they record the crucifixion by simply saying, "And there they crucified Him." There is no word of soldiers hammering the nails in His hands and feet. It is only after the resurrection that we read in the Gospels of Jesus pointing out the nail prints, first to the disciples (John 20:20) and then later to Thomas (20:24). Even in this detail, Jesus made the truth of David's lament true.

It was in the words of the same Psalm, 22, that Jesus found a vocabulary to express the inexpressible forsakenness of the three darkest hours of the cross. Even as all truth came together in Him, on Golgotha He held together all the suffering of the sin of the world. The cross on which He hung was a nexus where pain and healing intersected, where sin and salvation were held together until one exhausted itself against the other. Hanging there, Jesus gave exhausted voice to the laments of David.

The Echo of Jeremiah's Weeping

We saw that Jeremiah fulfilled a unique role by lamenting to God for the people and, at the same time, lamenting for God to the people. He was an intercessor of lament. It was a role that tore him apart.

Because of the Incarnation, in Jesus' eyes the tears of God and those of the people mingled and flowed together as well. He was the man of the sorrows of both the people and His Father. They came together, He held them together.

Even as Jeremiah wept over Jerusalem, so we see Jesus lamenting over the city in at least two different places. The first is Luke 13:34. In just three days, Jesus will enter Jerusalem for the last time. Along the way He receives a warning from the Pharisees to flee from Herod. Jesus responds to their warning by issuing a warning of His own. Calling Herod a "fox," He insists that He will continue on with His ministry of healing and casting out demons for two more days. On the third day, Jesus says, He will arrive in Jerusalem, "for surely no prophet can die outside of Jerusalem."

His statement about the prophets and Jerusalem prompts Jesus to lament for the city. He speaks of the desire of His heart to gather the children together, but the children of Israel were unwilling. Echoing the words of Jeremiah 22:5, Jesus pronounces that the house is desolate. Even as the Babylonians had come to make visible the truth that the first Temple was truly a wasteland, Jesus saw that the Romans would come some forty years in the future and actualize the spiritual devastation the priests and the people had already inflicted there.

The second passage, Luke 19:41-44, occurs just three days later. Jesus is making his so-called "triumphal entry" into Jerusalem, riding a colt, a sign that He was coming in peace. A small band of His followers circles around Him. The Passover crowd presses in as well. The Pharisees are disturbed by the adulation He is receiving and ask Jesus to rebuke his disciples. Jesus tells them it is hopeless because if the people were to keep quiet the stones would cry out.

Luke tells us that when Jesus saw the city He began to openly weep. "If only . . ." provides the forsaken tone of the lament. If only they had known. If only they had seen. But it has been hidden from their eyes as a result of their stubbornness. Jesus sees the detailed scene of the siege ramp that Titus will build. He sees, as Jeremiah saw, the suffering of the children. He doesn't move to "fix" it, instead He simply weeps.

Remembering what He said a moment before about the stones crying out, Jesus foresees one of the worst details: the Temple sacked and burned by Titus in AD 70, the Roman soldiers literally prying the stones apart to retrieve the melted gold from the Temple walls. Jesus sees it all, every detail, and bursts into tears. His tears, as well as many of His actual words, are Jeremiah's. The painful sense of having been rejected by His own people brings forth from Jesus the tears of God. But finally, Jesus weeps for Himself, for His own confusion and pain, and for His disappointed hopes for His people.

All the truth of what He saw and all the tears, part of the "all things" Paul promised would come together in Jesus' tearful eyes. In and through Him we now understand the Truth of His Incarnation because His life fleshed it out before us. Along with Him, the Man of Sorrows, we are invited to weep. He holds them together, both the truth and the tears, through lament.

CHAPTER 20

Hesed In-fleshed

"The Word became flesh and made his dwelling among us, . . . full of grace . . .[*hesed*]" (John 1:14). We have seen that *hesed* lies at the heart of every lament. The basis for the psalmists' prayer of protest is that God has acted in some way that is inconsistent with *hesed*. His enemy has triumphed or perhaps he is suffering with a disease. Job is a perfect paradigm. He cries out because he knows his suffering is unintelligible in light of who he believes God to be — namely, a God of *hesed*. You and I lament because we cannot understand how a God of *hesed* could possibly allow us to experience pain. The cause for all lament is an inconsistency between the perceived action of God and the revealed character of God as defined by the word *hesed*. It is the source of the complaint as well as the solution.

On the other side of lament, once we have exhausted ourselves against God, it is His *hesed* that holds on to us when we do not deserve it. *Hesed* causes Him to remain faithful in the face of our constant faithlessness. It is an expression of His grace.

When John seeks to spell out in Greek what his Hebrew mind knows is true about Jesus, time and time again he uses the word "grace," one of the principle equivalents of *hesed*. If we accept this kind of retrograde translation we can say that in 1:14 the Incarnate Word is full of *hesed*. Just two verses later John writes:

"From the fullness of his grace (*hesed*) we have all received one
blessing after another" (NIV).

The blessings we have received, one after the other, are undeserved, surprising blessings precisely because they are the result of the fullness of His
hesed. Grace and *hesed*, while not strictly equal, significantly overlap in their
meaning.

When we look at the ministry of Jesus, we see that a major part of it
was really devoted to teaching what *hesed* was all about. He told parable after
parable in an attempt to define it for his followers. *Hesed* is defined in the
Samaritan who shows mercy to someone who by rights should be treated like
an enemy (Luke 10:30-37). You might call it "enemy-love."

We witness it fleshed out in the silhouette of the father, standing against
the setting sun, expectantly waiting for his no-good son to return (Luke
15:11-32). When he finally does return he does not get what he deserves,
as the old equation would dictate. No, he gets what he decidedly does not
deserve through the grace (*hesed*) of his father. You might call this "unexpected favor."

It is made visible in the story of the farmer who outrageously pays the
late-comers the same wage as those who bore the heat of the day (Matthew
20:14). In this disturbing parable, Jesus is painting a portrait of a God who
is infuriatingly gracious to the slackers, regardless of their poor performance.
Jesus is trying to finally convince his listeners of One who is amazingly kind
to the ungrateful (Luke 6:35). You might call it "surprising grace."

You might choose any of a limitless number of words to call it by, for it
is an infinite, untranslatable word. Could Jesus' actual words in Matthew
5:7 have been, "Blessed are the ones who do *hesed* for they shall obtain *hesed*"
(Matthew 18:33-35)? Or a few verses later in 5:48, did Jesus say, "Do *hesed*
even as your Father does *hesed*"?

As Jesus defines *hesed* in His parables, the consistent theme is that
the person from whom we should expect nothing gives everything. The

Samaritan rescues the Jew, his enemy. The father forgives the ungrateful son. The farmer pays a day's wage for a few hours work. None of them were obliged to show mercy, yet each of them did.

Jesus' most powerful definition of *hesed* was the one He perfectly lived out. And, like His Father, His followers constantly thought Jesus was acting in ways that were inconsistent with this defining characteristic. Jesus most often failed to answer people's questions, like His Father in Job. They could not understand that because of His *hesed*, Jesus had not come to simply give them the answers they thought they needed, but to give them the one and only thing they truly did need, Himself. Why, they asked, would He let His friend Lazarus die? They could not understand that, because of His *hesed*, Jesus wanted to give Lazarus more than healing, He wanted to give him new life! Why, they wondered, did He not come down from the cross and save Himself? They could not understand that because of His *hesed* He would refuse to save Himself in order to save them. If *hesed* can be defined as "enemy-love," then the cross provides the final perfect and concrete definition. Paul writes in Romans 5:10, NIV:

> For if, when we were God's enemies, we were reconciled to him
> through the death of his Son.

It required the Incarnation to finally define that indefinable word, *hesed*. It could never have been contained by human words. It demanded the Incarnate Word to express all the infinite fullness of its meaning.[1]

CHAPTER 21

GOD'S PRESENCE "WITH US"

"AND THEY WILL CALL HIM IMMANUEL"—WHICH MEANS, "GOD WITH US" (Matthew 1:23, NIV). We saw earlier that the ultimate answer to all laments is not to be found in the specifics of what is lamented for. The true answer for a lament of disease is not ultimately a cure. The real solution for a lament of financial distress is never simply money. The answer is always found in the Presence of God. It is rarely what we ask for, but it is always what we ultimately need.

In the end of the book, God's answer to Job's loss is not getting his dead children back. Indeed he never gets them back. The answer, God's answer, is that Job gets God back. And Job's response, brought into focus by his suffering is clear: That is all he ever really needed. The same can be said for both David and Jeremiah and you and me.

The coming of Immanuel, "God with us," must be understood as the Father's answer to ages of expectant laments. But God did not send the Messiah as the sort of solution everyone expected. They wanted someone who would kill the Romans. Jesus, instead died for the Romans. They wanted someone who would give them answers. Jesus gave them Himself. What else but His Presence could have perfectly answered all our deepest needs? For though we could have never imagined it, what we thought we needed, solutions for the problems that caused our pain, would have never fixed the problem.

I have a pastor friend who was almost killed in a horrible car accident a few years ago. As he tells it, he was fortunate to be alive but was sadly paralyzed from the neck down.

In the hospital, the doctors placed him in one of those sandwich type contraptions that would allow his whole body to be turned over to prevent bed sores and encourage his otherwise poor circulation. Often this meant he would be left, face down, staring at the floor for hours, unable to move or even turn his head.

On one such evening, as he waited patiently for a nurse to come and rotate the bed, he sensed a presence enter the room. It was so real and palpable that he wrongly assumed it was the nurse, come to help him out of his helpless upside-down situation.

"Is that you?" he called out.

No answer.

Still positive that someone had entered the room, he asked again, "Is there anybody there?"

All at once, he said, he was given the awareness that the presence that had entered the hospital room was none other than Jesus Himself. But my friend saw nothing out of the ordinary, no bright light, no outline of an angelic figure. Only the certainty that in an extraordinary sense, Jesus had come to be with him. He had come in answer to my friend's angry prayers of lament.

"I can't tell you how long it lasted," he said. "It could have been a few minutes or a few hours." But in time he realized that this powerfully immediate experience was coming to an end.

And then it happened. My friend plunged into a desperate despair that he had never known before. "Please, please, don't leave me!" he shouted in tears. "I realized at that moment," he said, "that what I wanted most was not Jesus' provision of my healing. That desire had totally evaporated. All I wanted was His Presence."

"I will do anything," he cried, "Just don't leave!"

What we need most, though few of us will ever realize it with the depth and intensity of my friend, is never what we think we need. What we were created at the depths of our souls to need is only the Presence of God. It is the answer, as Jesus is the answer.

After the Resurrection, whenever Jesus spoke of His imminent departure to go and be with the Father, His disciples would inevitably lament, "Why can't you stay with us?"

Jesus' remarkable answer is found in John 14. There He resonates with their sorrow. "Don't let your hearts be troubled," He comforts. "I will not leave you comfortless. I will come to you."

The object of this wonderful promise is, of course, the Holy Spirit. By their very nature, it would be impossible for either God the Father or Jesus the Son to not be with us. So the Spirit, the Comforter, who comes today in response to all our laments, still provides the only answer that will ever be enough, whether we realize it or not.

Rarely does He move to solve the problem. Something else that we don't understand must be taking place. What lament would have us understand is that the answer is being graciously given: His Presence is always with us.

Lament is the path that takes us to the place where we discover that there is no complete answer to pain and suffering, only Presence. The language of lament gives a meaningful form to our grief by providing a vocabulary for our suffering and then offering it to God as worship. Our questions and complaints will never find individual answers (even as Job's questions were never fully answered). The only Answer is the dangerous, disturbing, comforting Presence, which is the true answer to all our questions and hopes.[1]

CHAPTER 22

The God-Forsaken God

"He was despised and rejected by men, a man of sorrows, and familiar with suffering. . . . Surely he took up our infirmities and carried our sorrows" (Isaiah 53:3-4, NIV). Even as you and I first came into the world hearing the laments of our Eve-cursed mothers, Jesus also was born with the sound of such pain echoing in His tiny ears. Tragically, those were not the only laments that heralded His coming into the world. Appropriately enough, it was Jeremiah, that other incarnation of lament, who heard ringing in his own ears some four hundred years earlier — the sound of suffering so intense that even he, who had spent so many of his words describing pain, struggled to find the words to describe it:

> Then what was said through the prophet Jeremiah was fulfilled:
> "A voice is heard in Ramah,
>   weeping and great mourning,
> Rachel weeping for her children
>   and refusing to be comforted,
> because they are no more." (Matthew 2:17-18, NIV)

"Rachel's children," all the infant boys of Bethlehem two years old and younger, were simply gone. As they lay lifeless in their mother's arms, their throats having been cut by Herod's soldiers, their mothers returned to the only language they knew in an attempt to describe their indescribable pain. We are told that they refused to be comforted, perhaps because they knew that comfort was not what they needed just yet. What their souls needed to survive, just as Job had survived his loss, was lament. So intense was their cry that it echoed back through time and found a sympathetic hearer in the weeping prophet, Jeremiah.

It was Isaiah who took up where Jeremiah left off in describing the lost years of Jesus' childhood. It only occurs to me just now that, except for Luke's precious but frustratingly brief account of the twelve-year-old Jesus misplaced in the Temple (Luke 2:41-52), this word from Isaiah is the only other description of His childhood we have.

> He grew up before him like a tender shoot,
>> and like a root out of dry ground.
> He had no beauty or majesty to attract us to him,
>> nothing in his appearance that we should desire him.
> He was despised and rejected by men,
>> a man of sorrows, and familiar with suffering.
> Like one from whom men hide their faces
>> he was despised, and we esteemed him not.
> Surely he took up our infirmities
>> and carried our sorrows.
> ISAIAH 53:2-4 (NIV)

The "tender shoot" that grew up in the lonely hills of Nazareth apparently looked nothing like what we expected, even as the young David's appearance revealed nothing special to Samuel. We did not seek Him out, says Isaiah — the truth is, we hid our faces from Him. And why so? Could it be because we did not want to look upon such a face so familiar with suffering, our suffering. We had seen enough of that in our own mirrors.

Please don't misunderstand me. I am not saying that Jesus' life was only sorrow and lament. There are precious moments in the Gospels when His ordinary face would light up and overflow with joy (see Luke 10:21). To have been fully human, it must have been so. But joy and sadness live closer together than any of us can imagine.

The ultimate coming together of sorrow and joy was experienced by Jesus on the cross. When He lamented, "Why have You forsaken me?" Jesus voiced all our laments. The heartbreaking truth is . . . God did forsake Him. Suspended over the "Place of the Skull," held there by Roman nails, hung the God-forsaken God. Their eternal unity impossibly broken, because God could not look upon the sin that Jesus became. The Life died there. But the Scriptures give us the reason, the motivation for Jesus' enduring the world's weight of sorrow:

> "Let us fix our eyes on Jesus, the author and perfecter of
> our faith, who for the *joy* set before him endured the cross."
> (Hebrews 12:2, NIV, emphasis added)

Amidst crushing sorrow and confusion, Jesus endured. He suffered with the disturbing clarity that only the hope of joy can give. There He exhausted Himself against the God Whose Presence was nowhere to be seen. Who at this moment, above all moments, seemed most inconsistent with His *hesed*. Earlier, in the Garden, Jesus had crossed the line from I to Thou with the words, "Not *my* will but *Thine* be done." On the cross He demonstrated it. Losing everything, He won for us the assurance of Presence. Jesus' death and resurrection once and for all should give us hope that we can never be forsaken, forgotten, or overlooked by God. He is Immanuel, the God who is ever with us. The God who is moved by our tears.

PART SIX

✦✦✦

CONCLUSIONS

CHAPTER 23

THE LOST LANGUAGE OF LAMENT

WITHIN EACH OF US LIES A HIDDEN HOLY OF HOLIES. LIKE THE ONE OF OLD, it can only be entered by a high priest, and then not without blood. Our laments are that most sacred place. And Jesus, the Man of Sorrows, is our high priest.

At every major turning point of His ministry, Jesus pours out His heart in lament — when He enters Jerusalem for the last time, when He experiences his final meal with the disciples, when He struggles with the Father in the Garden of Gethsemane, and most importantly, when He endures the suffering of the cross. Jesus understood the honesty represented in the life that knows how to lament. His life reveals that those who are truly intimate with the Father know they can pour out any hurt, disappointment, temptation, or even anger with which they struggle. Jesus spoke fluently the lost language of lament. He is our best hope of recovering this forgotten vocabulary.

Each time we refuse Him entrance to our holy place, every time we doggedly deny our sacred right of lament, we tell the world in effect that the cross has nothing to do with us. Without realizing it, we plug our ears so as not to hear Him lamenting for us to God, "Why have you forsaken me?" The "You" might then not be capitalized, referring to us, who have forsaken Jesus by our own inability to listen.

The truth is, all of us have felt forsaken. At the precise point when Jesus was most forsaken by God, He was being used the most by God. When He was lamenting God's perceived absence, something was being accomplished through His life that would save the world. It is often the same for us.

Jesus lamented for us all. Jesus still intercedes for us all. The best news of the Gospel is that because of Jesus, none of us will ever again, could ever again, be forsaken by God.

Jesus was forsaken for our sakes when He took upon Himself all our sin upon which God, with His pure eyes, could not look. For the only time in all eternity, God looked away from His Son. Jesus experienced the hell of His hidden face, so that if we come to Him, we will never be separated from God's Presence.

If it is true that we must be conformed to His image (Romans 8:29, NIV), then perhaps we must also learn to speak His lost language. If we must learn to never let go of God, then the best means, provided by the language of lament, must become ours as well. We must devote ourselves to finding it again. The promise of Jesus is that whatever was lost can be found once again, whether it was a sheep or a coin, a son, or even the language of lament. It was all the laments of ages past that brought Him finally into the world. It will be in response to our last long, loud lament, "Maranatha," that He will come back once more!

THE SWEET SCROLL OF LAMENT

Then I looked, and I saw a hand stretched out to me. In it was a scroll, which he unrolled before me. On both sides of it were written words of lament and mourning and woe.

And he said to me, "Son of man, eat what is before you, eat this scroll; then go and speak to the house of Israel." So I opened my mouth, and he gave me the scroll to eat.

Then he said to me, "Son of man, eat this scroll I am giving you and fill your stomach with it." So I ate it, and it tasted as sweet as honey in my mouth. (Ezekiel 2:9–3:3, NIV)

God presented a scroll to Ezekiel upon which was written a language that had been lost by the people of God. His call was to teach them once again the lament vocabulary of repentance. What he expected to be bitter turned out to be as "sweet as honey." His obedience in entering into lament, in allowing it to enter into him, would give shape and meaning to the rest of Ezekiel's life.

The prospect of seriously entering into biblical lament seems just as bitter to us today. Perhaps it should. Each of us holds in our hand such a scroll as was presented to Ezekiel. It is the Bible, which we have seen is so full of lament. Could it be that today He is inviting us to taste and see that what we imagine as bitter and foul tasting will lead us to a sweetness we would have never expected?

Enshrined in that scroll you are holding are the bitterest prayers of complaint. God knows we need to give them voice, learn their language, taste and discover to our surprise that they are sweeter than honey.

Pull Off the Clapboard

Where I live, in the South, people who move into newly restored rustic log homes consider themselves lucky. As you drive through the country you sometimes see them dotting the green landscape. Few people, however, realize the convoluted path that allowed so many genuinely historic log homes to survive two centuries and more to this present day.

When white settlers first came to this region in the late 1600s, the quickest form of shelter they could throw up was a log cabin. (Further west, where there were so few trees, settlers had to build their homes from sod.) Several trees would be felled and, if there was time, squared along their full length by means of an "adz." Then complicated interlocking notches were cut in the ends so that the logs could be stacked in square patterns that would eventually be roofed. The spaces between the logs would then be "chinked," with mud. It was quick to build, provided a relatively dry interior space that

could fend off the subtropical summer heat and, by means of a small fire-
place, could barely keep its desperately cold inhabitants from freezing in the
harsh winter. It was only seen by the settlers as a temporary, impoverished
kind of shelter.

As soon as the country became stable and safe, the people who lived in
these humble cabins would travel to the closest saw mill and buy as much
"clap board" as their still-poor means could afford. (The name "clap" refers
to the sound the boards would make in a strong wind when the square nails
that were supposed to hold them in place would come loose.) With this fancy
milled lumber, along with whitewash, the settlers would quickly cover up the
logs in an effort to make any passerby think that their log home was really a
more sophisticated and expensive timber frame house. Here lies the fortunate quirk of their pride. By covering up the apparent poverty of the humble
logs, they ended up preserving the "embarrassing" structures for two hundred
or more years, long enough for values to shift to where they are today, a time
in which a log home is seen as a sign of understated affluence and pride.

Where in the world is he going with this? you might be wondering. In the direction of a powerful parable, I hope.

There have existed, at various times in the history of our faith, periods
when followers of Jesus freely engaged in lament. These tended to be harsher
times of discrimination or even persecution. Lament provided a humble,
humbling structure to which they would flee amidst the heat of hatred and
the winter cold of isolation. It was not a necessarily beautiful place to go, but
often it was the *only* place to go.

Inevitably, those harsher times would pass by, or pass over like the angel
of death, and the faithful would return to more normal lives. As comfort
returned, they looked back on their lamentable struggles, not in psalmic formulas of remembrance, but with a certain embarrassment. Had they committed some secret sin to have deserved those hard times? And so they clapboarded
over their laments in an attempt to hide their former poverty of spirit. They
offered to the world a more proper "hymnody." Are you following me?

What if (and this is such an exciting "what if" my hands are trembling at the keyboard), what if we, you and I, began moving in the direction of pulling off the clapboard and restoring those ancient, humble dwellings of lament? What if we moved back into those darker interior spaces and learned to live again in the shadows of their simplicity? What if our value systems took such a biblical redirection that a life which included lament was seen to be a richer and not a poorer life? What if . . .

The End of Lament

Lament had its precise beginning in the garden. There was a high point along the journey when Jesus, the Presence and the Incarnation of *hesed*, joined us on the pathway. And now we see the promise of an end to lament.

Revelation describes the exact moment in history when the Presence of God will come crashing gloriously into history once more, undeniable and inescapable. As He is unveiled in the Apocalypse, so too is the plan of His *hesed* unfolded, like a scroll with many seals. The promises He made that were believed and accepted by His children are perfectly kept in undreamed-of glory.

"But," you are thinking, "Does Revelation not also speak of judgment, of fire and the casting out of unbelievers?"

What must be understood, in the light of God's Word, is that those who are cast out are the ones who refused His *hesed* and lived their lives in such a way as to say it was all ultimately a lie. They believed the primordial lie in the garden that God did not really act according to *hesed*, that His Presence was not a reality. In Revelation, we simply read of God's own sad pronouncement of a judgment these willful disbelievers have passed upon themselves.

"I am here for you," God said. "My Presence is real and true."

"You cannot be either," was their response.

"I am kind and compassionate. I love you," He spoke in His Word and through His own Son.

"You are none of these," they said with their lips and their lives.

Echoing Adam's intention in the garden, they say, "Our will be done!"

Revelation is an account of God's own "very well."

Nothing more can be done to save them because everything has already been done to save them. God has sent His own Son to die, to spell out His *hesed* with Jesus' own blood.

The long-awaited moment comes: "He will wipe every tear from their eyes." (Revelation 21:4;7:17, NIV)

The verb used for "to wipe" (εχαλεφφ) indicates more than just a Divine handkerchief blotting out tears. It is a fierce wiping out; it could almost be translated "stamping out." In the sense that a new police chief promises to wipe out crime, God promises He will wipe out tears for all time.[1]

Presence undeniable, *hesed* as immediate and palpable as the fresh air of the New Jerusalem. Lament is over forever. It comes to a crashing halt with the words:

"Behold, I make all things new." (Revelation 21:5, KJV)

In that moment, we will realize to our great joy that, all along, this journey of lament has been a journey toward the New Jerusalem. From the Garden of Eden, through the Garden of Gethsemane, past the Garden Tomb, through our own times of wrestling in our dark gardens, as we pass through the gates of the New Jerusalem, we leave our laments and forget once and for all the vocabulary of their pain and the syntax of their sorrows! Lament will become the faithful companion with whom we part ways when the journey comes to an end.

But wait. This remains a future destination. It gives reason for hope, the promise of God's Presence and the vindication of His *hesed*. This hope is meant to shape and give meaning to us in the twists and turns of the journey. But the future hope does not cancel out our need to lament now; in fact it accentuates our deep need to lament what remains. The promised hope makes the pain of the present journey more bearable.

Lament: The Hell of the Hidden Face of God

High and lifted up, You shrieked one single lament,

"Why have You forsaken me?"

As the Face You had always had in view
Vanished behind the dark clouds that surrounded You.
You entered into the hell of the hidden face of God,
And became that thing in me
He could not see because of His too holy eyes.

That song you had not the life to complete
Goes on to sing that He did not forever hide His face
From the afflicted One.
At some unspoken moment You became once more
The looked-upon One
And hell was over for You and me.

Sometimes I too look for that Face
You could not find.
And would cry out in your words,
But because You endured the Facelessness of that hell
Which is hell indeed,
Your cry could never be mine,
Must never be spoken by my groaning lips
For it is Your face I now, forever behold
And seeing it is Light and Hesed and unassailable Hope
And the certainty of faith that the still sometimes hidden Face
Will never mean hell to me

Appendices

A Biblical Chorus of Lamenters

GOD. He laments (is "grieved") for having created man (Genesis 6:6). God laments His people wanting another king besides Him (1 Samuel 8:7).

DAVID. He laments Saul and Jonathan (2 Samuel 1:17). David laments for Abner (2 Samuel 3:33). David laments for Absalom (2 Samuel 18:33).

JEREMIAH. Jeremiah composes laments for Josiah (2 Chronicles 35:25). He laments for God and the people (Jeremiah 12:1-4; 14:17-22; 20:7-18; 25:34-38; Lamentations 1-5).

EZRA. Ezra laments over the people's sins (9:6).

SOLOMON. He laments the meaninglessness of life (Ecclesiastes 1:1-11; 2:10-16; 4; 5:10-20; 6:7-11).

HEZEKIAH. He laments his disease (Isaiah 38:10-20).

ISAIAH. Isaiah laments the sufferings of the coming Savior (52:13–53:13).

EZEKIEL. He laments for the princes of Israel (Ezekiel 19). He laments for Tyre (27). He laments for Egypt (30). He laments for the pharaoh of Egypt (32).

DANIEL. He laments Israel's sins and appeals to God's *hesed* (Daniel 9:4-19).

AMOS. He laments the house of Israel (Amos 5:1-4).

JONAH. He laments in the belly of the whale (Jonah 2).

MICAH. He laments the destruction of Samaria (Micah 1:8-16).

HABAKKUK. He laments that God seems to be acting in a way inconsistent with *hesed* (Habakkuk 1:2-4,12–2:1).

ZECHARIAH. He laments the piercing of the Messiah (Zechariah 12:10-14).

MATTHEW. He records a lament for the innocents of Bethlehem (2:18, compare with Jeremiah 31:15).

JESUS. He pronounces a "barocha" on those who lament (Matthew 5:4), weeps over Lazarus (John 11:33,35), laments from the cross (Matthew 27:46), laments over Jerusalem (Luke 13:34).

PAUL. He laments the thorn in his flesh that will not be taken away. "My grace (*hesed*) is sufficient," replies God (2 Corinthians 12:7). Paul laments the cross (Philippians 2:6-8,9-11. "Therefore" represents the same kind of reversal we saw with the *vav* adversative.)

THE MARTYRS. The lament of those slain because of the Word of the Lord (Revelation 6:10).

A Selected List of Lament Psalms

3   A lament for the warrior. First Psalm of David.

5   Individual lament on the morning Temple service.

12   Isolation/abandonment by God.

13   Suffering = joy. Pain and praise. Desolation to delight. Presence =
         trust.

17   First psalm to be called a prayer.

22   The virtuous sufferer, a lament that is rooted in trust and faith. Not
         an accusation but a scream of confusion.

25   Isolation. Presence = trust.

26   Presence = trust. Fear of death.

28   A plea for help from illness.

35   "How Long?"

38   Lament for a grievously ill person.

40   Joy/suffering reversed, logically wrong.

42/43 A national psalm of suffering. Presence = hope.

52   Presence = trust.

55   God sustains.

56   Suffering = joy. Presence = trust.

59   Plea of an innocent man.

69   Suffering = joy. Represents every individual element of lament.

70/71 Suffering = joy (senior citizen).

74   What do you do when the shepherd has turned against the sheep?

79   "How Long?"

80   The persistent prayer of a desperate man to a deaf deity. A near-death psalm.

85   A new year's psalm.

88   Saddest psalm in the Psalter. Does not resolve, an embarrassment to conventional faith. Most hopeless of all psalms. The only time the words, "I am hopeless" appear in the Old Testament.

90   Lament of Moses, the only psalm of Moses. It speaks of death as sleep (as Jesus does).

102   Psalm of suffering.

103   The most exquisite psalm of praise.

109   Protesting innocence. Most vindictive of psalms, never used in Jewish liturgy for worship. Seems to contradict the gospel command to love our enemies.

137   A vengeance psalm, one of the most famous in the Bible. Justice in its most primitive form.

Communal complaints:
Psalms 9–10; 44; 60; 74; 77; 79; 80; 85; 89; 90; 108.

Individual complaints:
Psalms 6; 13; 22; 35; 39; 42–43; 88; 102.

Enemies:
Psalms 6; 9–10; 15; 22; 35; 42–42.

Sickness and disease:
Psalms 13; 22; 42–43; 102.

Journaling/Writing Your Own Lament

Journaling provides a wonderful means of prayer. By now, you have immersed yourself in the biblical laments to the degree that some of their themes and language have worked their way into your own prayer life. Perhaps more to the point, hopefully you have experienced a new sense of freedom before God. You have learned from lament that you can and should offer Him everything as an act of worship.

As you move toward prayer, don't force the issue. Perhaps there is no pressing need for you to lament just now. Maybe there is some deeper listening you need to do to your own life before you move into lament. Perhaps this would be a good time to examine your own exhaustion. Come with a willingness to open your life completely to the Holy Spirit, asking Him to place a finger on those scars that need to be offered up through lament. This is a process that always takes more time than you or I can imagine. As one of my friends says, "The head is miraculously fast but the heart is mysteriously slow." This is heart work, only accomplished by the help of the Spirit.

❖ As thoughts for lament do begin to surface, remember those qualities we saw in Job, David, Jeremiah, and especially Jesus. They existed in marvelous freedom before God. They possessed a stubborn refusal to turn away from God. They understood with their hearts as well as their minds that God's character was defined by *hesed*. They realized that, most of all, they needed Presence. Do you? Do I? As you write your own laments, describe what that yearning for Presence feels like in your own life.

❖ You may want to make use of the Formula of Remembrance we saw in so many laments. Ask yourself, "What has God done in my life that is worth remembering?" This question will move you in the direction of seeing the "worth-ship" of God for yourself.

❖ At some point, you will inevitably experience the "crossing of the line" we saw occurring through the *Vav* Adversative in the laments. Remember, this is not a formula, it is a form. The movement from "me-centeredness" to "God-centeredness" cannot be forced. It also is the Spirit's work. Let it happen on its own.

Finally, after it does take place, spend as much time as you can simply inhabiting this new place before the throne of God. Thank God for graciously sharing His Presence with you. It is an amazing and costly gift He gives: full access to the throne.

(For those of you who would like to go even deeper, we have prepared an Experience Guide, a structured ten-week study for individuals or groups, which includes more guidelines and questions for journaling on lament.)

Selected Extra-Biblical Laments

All-seeing Light and Eternal Life of all things, look upon my misery with Thine eye of mercy, and let Thine infinite power vouchsafe to limit out some portion of deliverance unto me, as unto Thee shall seem most convenient. But yet, O my God, I yield unto Thy will and joyfully embrace what sorrow Thou wilt have me suffer. Only thus much let me crave of Thee (let my craving, O Lord, be acceptable of Thee, since even that proceeds from Thee), let me crave even by the noblest title, which in my greatest affliction I may give myself, that I am Thy creature, and by Thy goodness (which is Thyself), that Thou wilt suffer some beam of Thy majesty so to shine into my mind, that it may still depend confidently on Thee — Amen.

Sir Phillip Sidney

Most merciful and gracious Father, I bless and magnify Thy name that Thou hast adopted me into the inheritance of sons and hast given me a portion of my elder Brother. Thou Who art the God of patience and consolation, strengthen me that I may bear the yoke and burden of the Lord, without any uneasy and useless murmurs and ineffective unwillingness. Lord, I am unable to stand under the cross, unable of myself, but be Thou pleased to ease this load by fortifying my spirit, that I may be strongest when I am weakest, and may be able to do and suffer every thing that Thou pleasest, through Christ Who strengtheneth me. Let me pass through the valley of tears, and the valley of the shadow of death with safety and peace, with a meek spirit, and a sense of the divine mercies, through Jesus Christ — Amen.

JEREMY TAYLOR (1613-1667)

O god, Who makest cheerfulness the companion of strength, but apt to take wings in time of sorrow, we humbly beseech Thee that if, in Thy sovereign wisdom, Thou sendest weakness, yet for Thy mercy's sake deny us not the comfort of patience. Lay not more upon us, O heavenly Father, than Thou wilt enable us to bear; and, since the fretfulness of our spirits is more hurtful than the heaviness of our burden, grant us that heavenly calmness which comes of owning Thy hand in all things, and patience in the trust that Thou doest all things well — Amen.

ROWLAND WILLIAMS

In Thee, O Lord God, I place my when hope and refuge; on Thee I rest all my tribulation and anguish; for I find all to be weak and inconstant, whatsoever I behold out of Thee. For many friends cannot profit, nor strong helpers assist, nor the books of the learned afford comfort, nor any place, however retired and lovely, give shelter, unless Thou Thyself doest assist, strengthen, console, instruct, and guard us. For all things that seem to belong to the attainment of peace and felicity, without Thee are nothing, and do bring in truth no felicity at all. Thou therefore art the Fountain of all that is good; and to hope in Thee above all things, is the strongest comfort of Thy servants. To Thee, therefore, do I lift up my eyes; in Thee, my God, the Father of mercies, do I put my trust — Amen.

THOMAS À KEMPIS

(Good for Depression)
Grant unto us, Almighty God, in a time of sore distress, the comfort of the forgiveness of our sins. In time of darkness give us blessed hope, in time of sickness of body give us quiet courage; and when the heart is bowed down,

and the soul is very heavy, and life is a burden, and pleasure a weariness, and the sun is too bright, and life too mirthful, then may that Spirit, the Spirit of the Comforter, come upon us, and after our darkness may there be the clear shining of the heavenly light; and so, being uplifted again by Thy mercy, we may pass on through this our mortal life with quiet courage, patient hope, and unshaken trust, hoping through Thy loving-kindness and tender mercy to be delivered from death into the large life of the eternal years. Hear us of Thy mercy, through Jesus Christ our Lord — Amen.

George Dawson

O Lord, Who orderest all things for us in infinite wisdom and love, Who knowest my weakness, and every beating and aching of my heart, blindly blind, I give myself unto Thy tender loving heart. Only give me grace to think, speak, act, feel, as shall please Thy love — Amen.

E. B. Pursey

O Lord, my God! The amazing horrors of darkness were gathered around me, and covered me all over, and I saw no way to go forth; I felt the depth and extent of the misery of my fellow-creatures separated from the Divine harmony, and it was heavier than I could bear, and I was crushed down under it; lifted up my hand, I stretched out my arm but there was none to help me; I looked round about, and was amazed. In the depths of misery, O Lord, I remembered that Thou art omnipotent; that I had called Thee Father; and I felt that I loved Thee, and I was made quiet in my will, and I waited for deliverance from Thee. Thou hadst pity upon me, when no man could help me; I saw that meekness under suffering was showed to us in the most affecting example of Thy Son, and Thou toughest me to follow Him and I said, "Thy will, O Father, be done!"

John Woolman (1720–1772)

(Sickness and Disease)

Eternal and most glorious God, suffer me not so to undervalue myself as to give away my soul, Thy soul, Thy dear and precious soul, for nothing; and all the world is nothing, if the soul must be given for it. Preserve therefore, my soul, O Lord, because it belongs to Thee, and preserve my body because it belongs to my soul. Thou alone dost steer my boat through all its voyage, but hast a more especial care of it, when it comes to a narrow current, or to a dangerous fall of waters. Thou hast a care of the preservation of my body in all the ways of my life; but, in the straits of death, open Thine eyes wider, and enlarge Thy Providence towards me so far that no illness or agony may shake and benumb the soul. Do Thou so make my bed in all my sickness that, being used to Thy and, I may content with any bed of Thy making — Amen.

JOHN DONNE (1573–1631)

(Suffering in General)

Remember, O most pitying Father, what this frail and feeble work of Thine hands can bear without fainting; nothing, indeed, for itself, but all things in Thee, if strengthened by Thy grace. Wherefore grant me strength, that I may suffer and endure; patience alone I ask. Lord, give me this and behold my heart is ready. O God, my heart is ready to receive whatsoever shall be laid upon me. Grant that in my patience I may possess my soul; to that end, may I often look upon the face of Christ Thy Son, that, as He hath suffered such terrible things in the flesh, I may endeavor to be armed with the same mind. Wherefore I commit my strength unto Thee, O Lord; for Thou art my Strength and my Refuge. Keep me, and bring me safely out of this trial when it shall please thee — Amen.

TREASURY OF DEVOTION (1869)

(Simplicity)

O God, who art the Author of love, and the Lover of pure peace and affection, let all who are terrified by fears, afflicted by poverty, harassed by tribulation, worn down by illness, be set free by Thine indulgent tenderness, raised up by amendment of life, and cherished by Thy daily compassion, through Jesus Christ our Lord — Amen.

CALLICAN SACRAMENTARY (800)

(For Justice)
O Lord, strengthen and support, I entreat Thee, all persons unjustly accused of underrated. Comfort them by the ever-present thought that Thou knowest the whole truth, and wilt in Thine own good time make their righteousness as clear as the light. Give them grace to pray for such as do them wrong, and hear and bless them when they pray — Amen.

CHRISTINA ROSSETTI

Holy Father, whose chosen way of manifesting Thyself to Thy children is by the discipline of trial and pain, we rejoice that we can turn to Thee in the midst of great anxiety, and commit all our troubles to Thy sure help. As Thou art with us in the sunlight, oh, be Thou with us in the cloud. In the path by which Thou guidest us, though it be through desert and stormy sea, suffer not our faith to fail, but sustain us by Thy near presence, and let the comforts which are in Jesus Christ fill our hearts with peace. And, O God, grant that the fiery trial which trieth us may not be in vain, but may lead us to a cheerful courage, and a holy patience; and let the patience have her perfect work, that we may be perfect and entire, wanting nothing, wholly consecrate to Thee, through Jesus Christ our Lord — Amen.

HENRY W. FOOTE

My God, by Whose loving Providence, sorrows, difficulties, trial, dangers, become means of grace, lessons of patience, channels of hope, grant us good will to use and not abuse those privileges; and, of Thy great goodness, keep us alive through this dying life, that out of death Thou mayest raise us up to immortality. For His sake Who is the Life, Jesus Christ our Lord — Amen.

CHRISTINA ROSSETTI

Lord! When I am in sorrow I think on Thee. Listen to the cry of my heart, and my sorrowful complaint. Yet, O Father, I would not prescribe to Thee when and how Thy help should come. I will willingly tarry for the hour which Thou Thyself hast appointed for my relief. Meanwhile strengthen me by Thy Holy Spirit; strengthen my faith, my hope, my trust; give me patience and resolution to bear my trouble; and let me at last behold the time when Thou wilt make me glad by Thy grace. Ah, my Father! Never yet hast Thou forsaken Thy children, forsake not me. Ever dost Thou give gladness unto me. Always dost Thou relieve the wretched, relieve me too, when and where and how Thou wilt. Unto Thy wisdom, love, and goodness, I leave it utterly — Amen.

J. F. STACK (1680–1756)

(Justice)

Thou Who art Love, and Who seest all the suffering, injustice and misery which reign in this world, have pity, we implore Thee, on the work of Thy hands. Look mercifully upon the poor, the oppressed, and all who are heavy laden with error, labour, and sorrow. Fill our hearts with deep compassion for those who suffer, and hasten the coming of Thy kingdom of justice and truth — Amen.

CELASIAN (492)

O God Almighty, Who to them that have no might increasest strength, strengthen us to do and suffer Thy good will and pleasure; through Jesus Christ — Amen.

CHRISTINA ROSSETTI

O Lord my God, be not Thou far from me; my God, have regard to help me; for there have risen up against me sundry thoughts, and great fears, afflicting my soul. How shall I pass through unhurt? How shall I break them to pieces? This is my hope, my one only consolation, to flee unto Thee in every tribulation, to trust in Thee, to call upon Thee from my inmost heart, and to wait patiently for Thy consolation — Amen.

Thomas à Kempis

Almighty and merciful God, Who art the Strength of the weak, the Refreshment of the weary, the Comfort of the sad, the Help of the tempted, the Life of the dying, the God of patience and of all consolation; Thou knowest full well the inner weakness of our nature, how we tremble and quiver before pain, and cannot bear the cross without Thy Divine help and support. Help me, then, O eternal and pitying God, help me to possess my soul in patience, to maintain unshaken hope in Thee, to keep that childlike trust which feels a Father's heart hidden beneath the cross; so shall I be strengthened with power according to Thy glorious might, in all patience and long-suffering; I shall be enabled to endure pain and temptation, and, in the very depth of my suffering, to praise Thee with a joyful heart — Amen.

Johann Habermann (1516–1590)

(Depression)

Ah, God! Behold my grief and care. Fain would I serve Thee with a glad and cheerful countenance, but I cannot do it. However much I fight and struggle against my sadness, I am too weak for this sore conflict. Help me in my weakness, O Thou mighty God! And give me Thy Holy Spirit to refresh and comfort me in my sorrow. Amid all my fears and griefs I yet know that I am then in life and death, and that nothing can really part me from Thee; neither things present, nor things to come, neither trial, no fear, nor pain. And therefore, O Lord, I will still trust in Thy grace. Thou wilt not send me away unheard. Sooner of later Thou wilt lift this burden from my heart, and put a new song in my lips; and I will praise Thy goodness and thank and serve Thee here and for evermore — Amen.

S. SHERETZ (1584–1639)

All of the above are from "Great Souls at Prayer" compiled by Mary W. Tileston, James Clarke and Co, Cambridge (1898).

THE LAMENTATION
(Old Version, 1562)

O Lord, turn not away Thy face
From him who lies prostrate
Lamenting sore his sinful life
Before Thy mercy gate;

Which gate Thou openest wide to those
That do lament their sins;
Shut not the gate against me, Lord,
But let me enter in.

So come I to Thy mercy-gate,
Where mercy doth abound,
Requiring mercy for my sin
To heal my deadly wound.

Mercy, good Lord, mercy I ask,
This is the total sum;
For mercy, Lord, is all my suit;
Lord, let Thy mercy come.

JOHN MARCKANT (1560)

SONNET THIRTY-SIX

The glorious revelations you've bestowed,
Ineffable displays of holy light,
Call forth my praise in sheer delight,
A foretaste of my heavenly abode.
Then why this ceaseless thorn, this painful goad
Of Satan? Why not spare me the pain, the blight
Of persecution, malice, danger's fright?
From what strange stream of love have nettles flowed?
    Sufficient is my grace for you: indeed,
    My power is perfected when you're weak,
    Will you for your own feeble prowess plead,
    When bankrupt weakness brings the strength you seek?
Now insults, hardships, weakness are my song,
My joy: for when I'm weak, then I am strong.

D. A. CARSON

(*Holy Sonnets from the Twentieth Century*, D.A.Carson, copyright 1994, Baker Books.
Used by permission.)

THERE IS A BALM IN GILEAD

Sometimes I feel discouraged,
And think my work's in vain,
But then the Holy Spirit
Revives my soul again
A long ways from home
There is a balm in Gilead,
To make the wounded whole,
There is a balm in Gilead,
To heal the sin-sick soul.

Sometimes I Feel Like a Motherless Child

Sometimes I feel like a motherless child
Sometimes I feel like a motherless child
Sometimes I feel like a motherless child
A long ways from home
A long ways from home
A long ways from home
A long ways from home
Sometimes I feel like I'm almost gone
Sometimes I feel like I'm almost gone
Sometimes I feel like I'm almost gone
A long ways from home
A long ways from home
A long ways from home
A long ways from home

Were You There?

Were you there when they crucified my Lord?
Were you there when they crucified my Lord?
Oh, sometimes it causes me to tremble, tremble, tremble.
Were you there when they crucified my Lord?
Were you there when they nailed Him to the cross?
Were you there when they pierced Him in the side?
Were there when the sun refused to shine?
Were you there when they laid Him in the tomb?

I Ain't Got Weary Yet

I ain't got weary yet
I ain't got weary yet
I been in the wilderness a mighty long time
And I ain't got weary yet
I been praying like Silas
I been preaching like Paul
I been walking with my Savior,
I been walking with the Lord,
I been in the wilderness a mighty long time
I ain't got weary yet

I Am a Poor Pilgrim of Sorrow

I am a poor pilgrim of sorrow,
I'm tossed in this wide world alone.
No hope have I for tomorrow;
I've started to make heaven my home.
Sometimes I am tossed and driven, Lord
Sometimes I don't know where to roam,
I've heard of city called Heaven;
I've started to make it my home.

APPENDIX E

Selected Davidic Laments

Book I
(Psalms 1-41)

Psalm 5 (NRSV)
(individual lament on the morning Temple service)

Trust in God for Deliverance from Enemies

TO THE LEADER: FOR THE FLUTES. A PSALM OF DAVID.

¹ Give ear to my words, O Lord;
  give heed to my sighing.
² Listen to the sound of my cry,
  my King and my God,
  for to you I pray.
³ O Lord, in the morning you hear my voice;
  in the morning I plead my case to you, and watch.
⁴ For you are not a God who delights in wickedness;
  evil will not sojourn with you.
⁵ The boastful will not stand before your eyes;
  you hate all evildoers.
⁶ You destroy those who speak lies;
  the Lord abhors the bloodthirsty and deceitful.

---

*I have attempted to indicate the occurrences of the adversative vav, the word *hesed*.

vav 7 But I, through the abundance of your steadfast love,(*hesed*)
> will enter your house,
I will bow down toward your holy temple
> in awe of you.
8 Lead me, O Lord, in your righteousness
> because of my enemies;
> make your way straight before me.

9 For there is no truth in their mouths;
> their hearts are destruction;
their throats are open graves;
> they flatter with their tongues.
10 Make them bear their guilt, O God;
> let them fall by their own counsels;
because of their many transgressions cast them out,
> for they have rebelled against you.

vav 11 But let all who take refuge in you rejoice;
> let them ever sing for joy.
Spread your protection over them,
> so that those who love your name may exult in you.
12 For you bless the righteous, O Lord;
> you cover them with favor as with a shield.

PSALM 13 (NRSV)

(Suffering = joy, pain, and praise, desolation to delight, Presence = trust. A "How long?" psalm.)

Prayer for Deliverance from Enemies
TO THE LEADER. A PSALM OF DAVID.

1 How long, O Lord? Will you forget me forever?
> How long will you hide your face from me?

² How long must I bear pain in my soul,

and have sorrow in my heart all day long?

How long shall my enemy be exalted over me?

³ Consider and answer me, O LORD my God!

Give light to my eyes, or I will sleep the sleep of death,

⁴ and my enemy will say, "I have prevailed";

my foes will rejoice because I am shaken.

vav ⁵ But I trusted in your steadfast love (*hesed*);

my heart shall rejoice in your salvation.

⁶ I will sing to the LORD,

because he has dealt bountifully with me.

PSALM 22 (NRSV)

(the virtuous suffer, a lament that is rooted in trust and faith, not an accusation but a scream of confusion)

Plea for Deliverance from Suffering and Hostility

TO THE LEADER: ACCORDING TO THE DEER

OF THE DAWN. A PSALM OF DAVID.

¹ My God, my God, why have you forsaken me?

Why are you so far from helping me, from the words of my groaning?

² O my God, I cry by day, but you do not answer;

and by night, but find no rest.

vav ³ Yet you are holy,

enthroned on the praises of Israel.

⁴ In you our ancestors trusted;

they trusted, and you delivered them.

⁵ To you they cried, and were saved;

in you they trusted, and were not put to shame.

⁶ But I am a worm, and not human;
>   scorned by others, and despised by the people.
⁷ All who see me mock at me;
>   they make mouths at me, they shake their heads;
⁸ "Commit your cause to the LORD; let him deliver —
>   let him rescue the one in whom he delights!"

⁹ Yet it was you who took me from the womb;
>   you kept me safe on my mother's breast.
¹⁰ On you I was cast from my birth,
>   and since my mother bore me you have been my God.
¹¹ Do not be far from me,
>   for trouble is near
>   and there is no one to help.

¹² Many bulls encircle me,
>   strong bulls of Bashan surround me;
¹³ they open wide their mouths at me,
>   like a ravening and roaring lion.

¹⁴ I am poured out like water,
>   and all my bones are out of joint;
my heart is like wax;
>   it is melted within my breast;
¹⁵ my mouthª is dried up like a potsherd,
>   and my tongue sticks to my jaws;
>   you lay me in the dust of death.

¹⁶ For dogs are all around me;
>   a company of evildoers encircles me.
My hands and feet have shriveled;

[17] I can count all my bones.

They stare and gloat over me;

[18] they divide my clothes among themselves,

and for my clothing they cast lots.

vav [19] But you, O Lord, do not be far away!

O my help, come quickly to my aid!

[20] Deliver my soul from the sword,

my life from the power of the dog!

[21] Save me from the mouth of the lion!

From the horns of the wild oxen you have rescued me.

[22] I will tell of your name to my brothers and sisters;

in the midst of the congregation I will praise you:

[23] You who fear the Lord, praise him!

All you offspring of Jacob, glorify him;

stand in awe of him, all you offspring of Israel!

[24] For he did not despise or abhor

the affliction of the afflicted;

he did not hide his face from me,

but heard when I cried to him.

[25] From you comes my praise in the great congregation;

my vows I will pay before those who fear him.

[26] The poor shall eat and be satisfied;

those who seek him shall praise the Lord.

May your hearts live forever!

[27] All the ends of the earth shall remember

and turn to the Lord;

and all the families of the nations

shall worship before him.

[28] For dominion belongs to the LORD,
    and he rules over the nations.

[29] To him, indeed, shall all who sleep in the earth bow down;
    before him shall bow all who go down to the dust,
    and I shall live for him.
[30] Posterity will serve him;
    future generations will be told about the Lord,
[31] and proclaim his deliverance to a people yet unborn,
    saying that he has done it.

PSALM 26 (NRSV)
(Presence = trust, fear of death)

Plea for Justice and Declaration of Righteousness
OF DAVID.

[1] Vindicate me, O LORD,
    for I have walked in my integrity,
    and I have trusted in the LORD without wavering.
[2] Prove me, O LORD, and try me;
    test my heart and mind.
[3] For your steadfast love is before my eyes,
    and I walk in faithfulness to you.

[4] I do not sit with the worthless,
    nor do I consort with hypocrites;
[5] I hate the company of evildoers,
    and will not sit with the wicked.

[6] I wash my hands in innocence,
    and go around your altar, O LORD,

[7] singing aloud a song of thanksgiving,
     and telling all your wondrous deeds.

[8] O LORD, I love the house in which you dwell,
     and the place where your glory abides.
[9] Do not sweep me away with sinners,
     nor my life with the bloodthirsty,
[10] those in whose hands are evil devices,
     and whose right hands are full of bribes.

vav [11] But as for me, I walk in my integrity;
     redeem me, and be gracious to me.
[12] My foot stands on level ground;
     in the great congregation I will bless the LORD.

PSALM 28 (NRSV)
(a plea for help from illness. Note Psalm 30, a prayer of thanksgiving for recovery from illness)

Prayer for Help and Thanksgiving for It
OF DAVID.

[1] To you, O LORD, I call;
     my rock, do not refuse to hear me,
for if you are silent to me,
     I shall be like those who go down to the Pit.
[2] Hear the voice of my supplication,
     as I cry to you for help,
as I lift up my hands
     toward your most holy sanctuary.

[3] Do not drag me away with the wicked,
     with those who are workers of evil,

who speak peace with their neighbors,
>   while mischief is in their hearts.
4 Repay them according to their work,
>   and according to the evil of their deeds;
repay them according to the work of their hands;
>   render them their due reward.
5 Because they do not regard the works of the LORD,
>   or the work of his hands,
he will break them down and build them up no more.

6 Blessed be the LORD,
>   for he has heard the sound of my pleadings.
7 The LORD is my strength and my shield;
>   in him my heart trusts;
so I am helped, and my heart exults,
>   and with my song I give thanks to him.

8 The LORD is the strength of his people;
>   he is the saving refuge of his anointed.
9 O save your people, and bless your heritage;
>   be their shepherd, and carry them forever.

PSALM 31 (NRSV)

Prayer and Praise for Deliverance from Enemies
TO THE LEADER. A PSALM OF DAVID.

1 In you, O LORD, I seek refuge;
>   do not let me ever be put to shame;
>   in your righteousness deliver me.
2 Incline your ear to me; rescue me speedily.
>   Be a rock of refuge for me, a strong fortress to save me.

³ You are indeed my rock and my fortress;
  for your name's sake lead me and guide me,
⁴ take me out of the net that is hidden for me,
  for you are my refuge.
⁵ Into your hand I commit my spirit;
  you have redeemed me, O LORD, faithful God.

ᵛᵃᵛ ⁶ You hate those who pay regard to worthless idols,
  but I trust in the LORD.
⁷ I will exult and rejoice in your steadfast love, (*hesed?*)
  because you have seen my affliction;
  you have taken heed of my adversities,
⁸ and have not delivered me into the hand of the enemy;
  you have set my feet in a broad place.

⁹ Be gracious to me, O LORD, for I am in distress;
  my eye wastes away from grief,
  my soul and body also.
¹⁰ For my life is spent with sorrow,
  and my years with sighing;
my strength fails because of my misery,
  and my bones waste away.

¹¹ I am the scorn of all my adversaries,
  a horror to my neighbors,
an object of dread to my acquaintances;
  those who see me in the street flee from me.
¹² I have passed out of mind like one who is dead;
  I have become like a broken vessel.
¹³ For I hear the whispering of many —
  terror all around! —

as they scheme together against me,

    as they plot to take my life.

^{vav 14} But I trust in you, O LORD;

    I say, "You are my God."

¹⁵ My times are in your hand;

    deliver me from the hand of my enemies and persecutors.

¹⁶ Let your face shine upon your servant;

    save me in your steadfast love.

¹⁷ Do not let me be put to shame, O LORD,

    for I call on you;

let the wicked be put to shame;

    let them go dumbfounded to Sheol.

¹⁸ Let the lying lips be stilled

    that speak insolently against the righteous

    with pride and contempt.

¹⁹ O how abundant is your goodness

    that you have laid up for those who fear you,

and accomplished for those who take refuge in you,

    in the sight of everyone!

²⁰ In the shelter of your presence you hide them

    from human plots;

you hold them safe under your shelter

    from contentious tongues.

²¹ Blessed be the LORD,

    for he has wondrously shown his steadfast love to me

    when I was beset as a city under seige.

^{vav 22} I had said in my alarm,

    "I am driven far from your sight."

But you heard my supplications
>   when I cried out to you for help.

23 Love the LORD, all you his saints.
>   The LORD preserves the faithful,
>   but abundantly repays the one who acts haughtily.
24 Be strong, and let your heart take courage,
>   all you who wait for the LORD.

PSALM 38 (NRSV)

A Penitent Sufferer's Plea for Healing

A PSALM OF DAVID, FOR THE MEMORIAL OFFERING.

1 O Lord, do not rebuke me in your anger,
>   or discipline me in your wrath.
2 For your arrows have sunk into me,
>   and your hand has come down on me.

3 There is no soundness in my flesh
>   because of your indignation;
there is no health in my bones
>   because of my sin.
4 For my iniquities have gone over my head;
>   they weigh like a burden too heavy for me.

5 My wounds grow foul and fester
>   because of my foolishness;
6 I am utterly bowed down and prostrate;
>   all day long I go around mourning.
7 For my loins are filled with burning,
>   and there is no soundness in my flesh.

⁸ I am utterly spent and crushed;
  I groan because of the tumult of my heart.

⁹ O Lord, all my longing is known to you;
  my sighing is not hidden from you.
¹⁰ My heart throbs, my strength fails me;
  as for the light of my eyes — it also has gone from me.
¹¹ My friends and companions stand aloof from my affliction,
  and my neighbors stand far off.

¹² Those who seek my life lay their snares;
  those who seek to hurt me speak of ruin,
  and meditate treachery all day long.

¹³ But I am like the deaf, I do not hear;
  like the mute, who cannot speak.
¹⁴ Truly, I am like one who does not hear,
  and in whose mouth is no retort.

vav ¹⁵ But it is for you, O Lord, that I wait;
  it is you, O Lord my God, who will answer.
¹⁶ For I pray, "Only do not let them rejoice over me,
  those who boast against me when my foot slips."

¹⁷ For I am ready to fall,
  and my pain is ever with me.
¹⁸ I confess my iniquity;
  I am sorry for my sin.
¹⁹ Those who are my foes without cause are mighty,
  and many are those who hate me wrongfully.
²⁰ Those who render me evil for good
  are my adversaries because I follow after good.

²¹ Do not forsake me, O LORD;

    O my God, do not be far from me;

²² make haste to help me,

    O Lord, my salvation.

PSALM 39 (NRSV)

Prayer for Wisdom and Forgiveness

TO THE LEADER: TO JEDUTHUN. A PSALM OF DAVID.

¹ I said, "I will guard my ways

    that I may not sin with my tongue;

I will keep a muzzle on my mouth

    as long as the wicked are in my presence."

² I was silent and still;

    I held my peace to no avail;

my distress grew worse,

    ³ my heart became hot within me.

While I mused, the fire burned;

    then I spoke with my tongue:

⁴ "LORD, let me know my end,

    and what is the measure of my days;

    let me know how fleeting my life is.

⁵ You have made my days a few handbreadths,

    and my lifetime is as nothing in your sight.

Surely everyone stands as a mere breath.   *Selah*

    ⁶ Surely everyone goes about like a shadow.

Surely for nothing they are in turmoil;

    they heap up, and do not know who will gather.

⁷ "And now, O Lord, what do I wait for?

    My hope is in you.

⁸ Deliver me from all my transgressions.

    Do not make me the scorn of the fool.

⁹ I am silent; I do not open my mouth,

    for it is you who have done it.

¹⁰ Remove your stroke from me;

    I am worn down by the blows of your hand.

¹¹ "You chastise mortals

    in punishment for sin,

consuming like a moth what is dear to them;

    surely everyone is a mere breath.   *Selah*

¹² "Hear my prayer, O LORD,

    and give ear to my cry;

    do not hold your peace at my tears.

For I am your passing guest,

    an alien, like all my forebears.

¹³ Turn your gaze away from me, that I may smile again,

    before I depart and am no more."

BOOK II

(PSALMS 42–72)

PSALM 51 (NRSV)

Prayer for Cleansing and Pardon

TO THE LEADER. A PSALM OF DAVID, WHEN THE PROPHET NATHAN CAME
TO HIM, AFTER HE HAD GONE IN TO BATHSHEBA.

¹ Have mercy on me, O God, according to your steadfast love (*hesed*);

    according to your abundant mercy blot out my transgressions.

[2] Wash me thoroughly from my iniquity,
    and cleanse me from my sin.
[3] For I know my transgressions,
    and my sin is ever before me.
[4] Against you, you alone, have I sinned,
    and done what is evil in your sight,
so that you are justified in your sentence
    and blameless when you pass judgment.
[5] Indeed, I was born guilty,
    a sinner when my mother conceived me.

[6] You desire truth in the inward being;
    therefore teach me wisdom in my secret heart.
[7] Purge me with hyssop, and I shall be clean;
    wash me, and I shall be whiter than snow.
[8] Let me hear joy and gladness;
    let the bones that you have crushed rejoice.
[9] Hide your face from my sins,
    and blot out all my iniquities.

[10] Create in me a clean heart, O God,
    and put a new and right spirit within me.
[11] Do not cast me away from your presence,
    and do not take your holy spirit from me.
[12] Restore to me the joy of your salvation,
    and sustain in me a willing spirit.

[13] Then I will teach transgressors your ways,
    and sinners will return to you.
[14] Deliver me from bloodshed, O God,
    O God of my salvation,
    and my tongue will sing aloud of your deliverance.

¹⁵ O Lord, open my lips,

    and my mouth will declare your praise.

¹⁶ For you have no delight in sacrifice;

    if I were to give a burnt offering, you would not be pleased.

¹⁷ The sacrifice acceptable to God is a broken spirit;

    a broken and contrite heart, O God, you will not despise.

¹⁸ Do good to Zion in your good pleasure;

    rebuild the walls of Jerusalem,

¹⁹ then you will delight in right sacrifices,

    in burnt offerings and whole burnt offerings;

    then bulls will be offered on your altar.

Psalm 52 (nrsv)

Judgment on the Deceitful

TO THE LEADER. A MASKIL OF DAVID, WHEN DOEG THE EDOMITE CAME

TO SAUL AND SAID TO HIM, "DAVID HAS COME

TO THE HOUSE OF AHIMELECH."

¹ Why do you boast, O mighty one,

    of mischief done against the godly?

    All day long² you are plotting destruction.

Your tongue is like a sharp razor,

    you worker of treachery.

³ You love evil more than good,

    and lying more than speaking the truth.   *Selah*

⁴ You love all words that devour,

    O deceitful tongue.

ᵛᵃᵛ ⁵ But God will break you down forever;

    he will snatch and tear you from your tent;

    he will uproot you from the land of the living.   *Selah*

⁶ The righteous will see, and fear,
    and will laugh at the evildoer, saying,
⁷ "See the one who would not take
    refuge in God,
but trusted in abundant riches,
    and sought refuge in wealth!"

ᵛᵃᵛ ⁸ But I am like a green olive tree
    in the house of God.
I trust in the steadfast love (*hesed*) of God
    forever and ever.
⁹ I will thank you forever,
    because of what you have done.
In the presence of the faithful
    I will proclaim your name, for it is good.

PSALM 54 (NRSV)

Prayer for Vindication

TO THE LEADER: WITH STRINGED INSTRUMENTS. A MASKIL OF DAVID,
WHEN THE ZIPHITES WENT AND TOLD SAUL,
"DAVID IS IN HIDING AMONG US."

¹ Save me, O God, by your name,
    and vindicate me by your might.
² Hear my prayer, O God;
    give ear to the words of my mouth.

³ For the insolent have risen against me,
    the ruthless seek my life;
    they do not set God before them.   *Selah*

^{vav} ⁴ But surely, God is my helper;
>   the Lord is the upholder of my life.
⁵ He will repay my enemies for their evil.
>   In your faithfulness, put an end to them.

⁶ With a freewill offering I will sacrifice to you;
>   I will give thanks to your name, O LORD, for it is good.
⁷ For he has delivered me from every trouble,
>   and my eye has looked in triumph on my enemies.

PSALM 55 (NRSV)
David's wilderness experience

Complaint About a Friend's Treachery

TO THE LEADER: WITH STRINGED INSTRUMENTS.

A MASKIL OF DAVID.

¹ Give ear to my prayer, O God;
>   do not hide yourself from my supplication.
² Attend to me, and answer me;
>   I am troubled in my complaint.
I am distraught³ by the noise of the enemy,
>   because of the clamor of the wicked.
For they bring trouble upon me,
>   and in anger they cherish enmity against me.

⁴ My heart is in anguish within me,
>   the terrors of death have fallen upon me.
⁵ Fear and trembling come upon me,
>   and horror overwhelms me.
⁶ And I say, "O that I had wings like a dove!
>   I would fly away and be at rest;

⁷ truly, I would flee far away;

    I would lodge in the wilderness;   *Selah*

⁸ I would hurry to find a shelter for myself

    from the raging wind and tempest."

⁹ Confuse, O Lord, confound their speech;

    for I see violence and strife in the city.

¹⁰ Day and night they go around it

    on its walls,

and iniquity and trouble are within it;

    ¹¹ ruin is in its midst;

oppression and fraud

    do not depart from its marketplace.

¹² It is not enemies who taunt me —

    I could bear that;

it is not adversaries who deal insolently with me —

    I could hide from them.

¹³ But it is you, my equal,

    my companion, my familiar friend,

¹⁴ with whom I kept pleasant company;

    we walked in the house of God with the throng.

¹⁵ Let death come upon them;

    let them go down alive to Sheol;

    for evil is in their homes and in their hearts.

vav ¹⁶ But I call upon God,

    and the Lord will save me.

¹⁷ Evening and morning and at noon

    I utter my complaint and moan,

    and he will hear my voice.

[18] He will redeem me unharmed
  from the battle that I wage,
  for many are arrayed against me.
[19] God, who is enthroned from of old,   *Selah*
  will hear, and will humble them —
  because they do not change, and do not fear God.

[20] My companion laid hands on a friend
  and violated a covenant with me
[21] with speech smoother than butter,
  but with a heart set on war;
with words that were softer than oil,
  but in fact were drawn swords.

[22] Cast your burden on the LORD, and he will sustain you;
  he will never permit the righteous to be moved.
[23] But you, O God, will cast them down
  into the lowest pit;
the bloodthirsty and treacherous
  shall not live out half their days.
But I will trust in you.

PSALM 56 (NRSV)

Trust in God Under Persecution

TO THE LEADER: ACCORDING TO THE DOVE ON FAR-OFF
TEREBINTHS. OF DAVID. A MIKTAM, WHEN THE
PHILISTINES SEIZED HIM IN GATH.

[1] Be gracious to me, O God, for people trample on me;
  all day long foes oppress me;
[2] my enemies trample on me all day long,
  for many fight against me.

O Most High,[3] when I am afraid,

 I put my trust in you.

[4] In God, whose word I praise,

  in God I trust; I am not afraid;

  what can flesh do to me?

[5] All day long they seek to injure my cause;

  all their thoughts are against me for evil.

[6] They stir up strife, they lurk,

  they watch my steps.

As they hoped to have my life,

  so repay them for their crime;

  in wrath cast down the peoples, O God!

[8] You have kept count of my tossings;

  put my tears in your bottle.

  Are they not in your record?

[9] Then my enemies will retreat

  in the day when I call.

  This I know, that God is for me.

[10] In God, whose word I praise,

  in the Lord, whose word I praise,

[11] in God I trust; I am not afraid.

  What can a mere mortal do to me?

[12] My vows to you I must perform, O God;

  I will render thank offerings to you.

[13] For you have delivered my soul from death,

  and my feet from falling,

so that I may walk before God

  in the light of life.

Psalm 59 (nrsv)

Prayer for Deliverance from Enemies

TO THE LEADER: DO NOT DESTROY. OF DAVID. A MIKTAM, WHEN SAUL
ORDERED HIS HOUSE TO BE WATCHED IN ORDER TO KILL HIM.

¹ Deliver me from my enemies, O my God;
   protect me from those who rise up against me.
² Deliver me from those who work evil;
   from the bloodthirsty save me.

³ Even now they lie in wait for my life;
   the mighty stir up strife against me.
For no transgression or sin of mine, O Lord,
   ⁴for no fault of mine, they run and make ready.

Rouse yourself, come to my help and see!
   ⁵You, Lord God of hosts, are God of Israel.
Awake to punish all the nations;
   spare none of those who treacherously plot evil.   *Selah*

⁶ Each evening they come back,
   howling like dogs
   and prowling about the city.
⁷ There they are, bellowing with their mouths,
   with sharp words on their lips —
   for "Who," they think, "will hear us?"

ᵛᵃᵛ ⁸ But you laugh at them, O Lord;
   you hold all the nations in derision.
⁹ O my strength, I will watch for you;
   for you, O God, are my fortress.

[10] My God in his steadfast love (*hesed*) will meet me; my God will let me
   look in triumph on my enemies.
[11] Do not kill them, or my people may forget; make them totter by your
   power, and bring them down, O Lord, our shield.
[12] For the sin of their mouths, the words of their lips, let them be trapped in
   their pride.
For the cursing and lies that they utter,
   [13] consume them in wrath; consume them until they are no more.
Then it will be known to the ends of the earth
   that God rules over Jacob.   *Selah*

[14] Each evening they come back,
   howling like dogs
   and prowling about the city.
[15] They roam about for food,
   and growl if they do not get their fill.

vav [16] But I will sing of your might;
   I will sing aloud of your steadfast love (*hesed*) in the morning.
For you have been a fortress for me
   and a refuge in the day of my distress.
[17] O my strength, I will sing praises to you,
   for you, O God, are my fortress,
   the God who shows me steadfast love.

PSALM 60 (NRSV)

Prayer for National Victory After Defeat
(*Cp Ps 108.6-13*)

TO THE LEADER: ACCORDING TO THE LILY OF THE COVENANT. A MIKTAM

OF DAVID; FOR INSTRUCTION; WHEN HE STRUGGLED WITH ARAM

NAHARAIM AND WITH ARAM-ZOBAH, AND WHEN JOAB ON HIS RETURN
KILLED TWELVE THOUSAND EDOMITES IN THE VALLEY OF SALT.

¹ O God, you have rejected us, broken our defenses;
    you have been angry; now restore us!
² You have caused the land to quake; you have torn it open;
    repair the cracks in it, for it is tottering.
³ You have made your people suffer hard things;
    you have given us wine to drink that made us reel.

⁴ You have set up a banner for those who fear you,
    to rally to it out of bowshot.   *Selah*
⁵ Give victory with your right hand, and answer us,
    so that those whom you love may be rescued.

⁶ God has promised in his sanctuary:
    "With exultation I will divide up Shechem,
    and portion out the Vale of Succoth.
⁷ Gilead is mine, and Manasseh is mine;
    Ephraim is my helmet;
    Judah is my scepter.
⁸ Moab is my washbasin;
    on Edom I hurl my shoe;
    over Philistia I shout in triumph."

⁹ Who will bring me to the fortified city?
    Who will lead me to Edom?
¹⁰ Have you not rejected us, O God?
    You do not go out, O God, with our armies.
¹¹ O grant us help against the foe,
    for human help is worthless.
¹² With God we shall do valiantly;
    it is he who will tread down our foes.

PSALM 64 (NRSV)

Prayer for Protection from Enemies
TO THE LEADER. A PSALM OF DAVID.

[1] Hear my voice, O God, in my complaint;
　preserve my life from the dread enemy.
[2] Hide me from the secret plots of the wicked,
　from the scheming of evildoers,
[3] who whet their tongues like swords,
　who aim bitter words like arrows,
[4] shooting from ambush at the blameless;
　they shoot suddenly and without fear.
[5] They hold fast to their evil purpose;
　they talk of laying snares secretly,
thinking, "Who can see us?
　[6] Who can search out our crimes?
We have thought out a cunningly conceived plot."
　For the human heart and mind are deep.

vav [7] But God will shoot his arrow at them;
　they will be wounded suddenly.
[8] Because of their tongue he will bring them to ruin;
　all who see them will shake with horror.
[9] Then everyone will fear;
　they will tell what God has brought about,
　and ponder what he has done.

[10] Let the righteous rejoice in the LORD
　and take refuge in him.
Let all the upright in heart glory.

Psalm 69 (nrsv)

Prayer for Deliverance from Persecution
TO THE LEADER: ACCORDING TO LILIES. OF DAVID.

¹ Save me, O God,
    for the waters have come up to my neck.
² I sink in deep mire,
    where there is no foothold;
I have come into deep waters,
    and the flood sweeps over me.
³ I am weary with my crying;
    my throat is parched.
My eyes grow dim
    with waiting for my God.

⁴ More in number than the hairs of my head
    are those who hate me without cause;
many are those who would destroy me,
    my enemies who accuse me falsely.
What I did not steal
    must I now restore?
⁵ O God, you know my folly;
    the wrongs I have done are not hidden from you.

⁶ Do not let those who hope in you be put to shame because of me,
    O Lord God of hosts;
do not let those who seek you be dishonored because of me,
    O God of Israel.
⁷ It is for your sake that I have borne reproach,
    that shame has covered my face.
⁸ I have become a stranger to my kindred,
    an alien to my mother's children.

⁹ It is zeal for your house that has consumed me;

the insults of those who insult you have fallen on me.

¹⁰ When I humbled my soul with fasting,

they insulted me for doing so.

¹¹ When I made sackcloth my clothing,

I became a byword to them.

¹² I am the subject of gossip for those who sit in the gate,

and the drunkards make songs about me.

vav ¹³ But as for me, my prayer is to you, O Lord.

At an acceptable time, O God,

in the abundance of your steadfast love, answer me.

With your faithful help¹⁴ rescue me

from sinking in the mire;

let me be delivered from my enemies

and from the deep waters.

¹⁵ Do not let the flood sweep over me,

or the deep swallow me up,

or the Pit close its mouth over me.

¹⁶ Answer me, O Lord, for your steadfast love (*hesed*) is good;

according to your abundant mercy, turn to me.

¹⁷ Do not hide your face from your servant,

for I am in distress — make haste to answer me.

¹⁸ Draw near to me, redeem me,

set me free because of my enemies.

¹⁹ You know the insults I receive,

and my shame and dishonor;

my foes are all known to you.

²⁰ Insults have broken my heart,
    so that I am in despair.
I looked for pity, but there was none;
    and for comforters, but I found none.
²¹ They gave me poison for food,
    and for my thirst they gave me vinegar to drink.
²² Let their table be a trap for them,
    a snare for their allies.
²³ Let their eyes be darkened so that they cannot see,
    and make their loins tremble continually.
²⁴ Pour out your indignation upon them,
    and let your burning anger overtake them.
²⁵ May their camp be a desolation;
    let no one live in their tents.
²⁶ For they persecute those whom you have struck down,
    and those whom you have wounded, they attack still more.
²⁷ Add guilt to their guilt;
    may they have no acquittal from you.
²⁸ Let them be blotted out of the book of the living;
    let them not be enrolled among the righteous.
²⁹ But I am lowly and in pain;
    let your salvation, O God, protect me.

³⁰ I will praise the name of God with a song;
    I will magnify him with thanksgiving.
³¹ This will please the LORD more than an ox
    or a bull with horns and hoofs.
³² Let the oppressed see it and be glad;
    you who seek God, let your hearts revive.
³³ For the LORD hears the needy,
    and does not despise his own that are in bonds.

³⁴ Let heaven and earth praise him,

    the seas and everything that moves in them.

³⁵ For God will save Zion

    and rebuild the cities of Judah;

and his servants shall live there and possess it;

    ³⁶ the children of his servants shall inherit it,

    and those who love his name shall live in it.

PSALM 70 (NRSV)

Prayer for Deliverance from Enemies
(Psalm 40:13-17)

TO THE LEADER. OF DAVID, FOR THE MEMORIAL OFFERING.

¹ Be pleased, O God, to deliver me.

    O LORD, make haste to help me!

² Let those be put to shame and confusion

    who seek my life.

Let those be turned back and brought to dishonor

    who desire to hurt me.

³ Let those who say, "Aha, Aha!"

    turn back because of their shame.

⁴ Let all who seek you

    rejoice and be glad in you.

Let those who love your salvation

    say evermore, "God is great!"

⁵ But I am poor and needy;

    hasten to me, O God!

You are my help and my deliverer;

    O LORD, do not delay!

BOOK III

(PSALMS 73-89)

PSALM 86 (NRSV)

Supplication for Help Against Enemies

A PRAYER OF DAVID.

¹ Incline your ear, O LORD, and answer me,
> for I am poor and needy.
² Preserve my life, for I am devoted to you;
> save your servant who trusts in you.
You are my God;³ be gracious to me, O Lord,
> for to you do I cry all day long.
⁴ Gladden the soul of your servant,
> for to you, O Lord, I lift up my soul.
⁵ For you, O Lord, are good and forgiving,
> abounding in steadfast love (*hesed*) to all who call on you.
⁶ Give ear, O LORD, to my prayer;
> listen to my cry of supplication.
⁷ In the day of my trouble I call on you,
> for you will answer me.

⁸ There is none like you among the gods, O Lord,
> nor are there any works like yours.
⁹ All the nations you have made shall come
> and bow down before you, O Lord,
> and shall glorify your name.
¹⁰ For you are great and do wondrous things;
> you alone are God.

¹¹ Teach me your way, O LORD,

that I may walk in your truth;

give me an undivided heart to revere your name.

¹² I give thanks to you, O Lord my God, with my whole heart,

and I will glorify your name forever.

¹³ For great is your steadfast love toward me;

you have delivered my soul from the depths of Sheol.

¹⁴ O God, the insolent rise up against me;

a band of ruffians seeks my life,

and they do not set you before them.

vav ¹⁵ But you, O Lord, are a God merciful and gracious,

slow to anger and abounding in steadfast love (*hesed*) and faithfulness.

¹⁶ Turn to me and be gracious to me;

give your strength to your servant;

save the child of your serving girl.

¹⁷ Show me a sign of your favor,

so that those who hate me may see it and be put to shame,

because you, LORD, have helped me and comforted me.

BOOK V

(PSALMS 107-150)

PSALM 109 (NRSV)

(The most vindictive psalm, never used in Jewish liturgy for worship, seems to contradict the gospel command to love our enemy. There is nothing else I can do with my sin but take it to God.)

Prayer for Vindication and Vengeance
TO THE LEADER. OF DAVID. A PSALM.

¹ Do not be silent, O God of my praise.

² For wicked and deceitful mouths are opened against me,

 speaking against me with lying tongues.

³ They beset me with words of hate,

 and attack me without cause.

⁴ In return for my love they accuse me,

 even while I make prayer for them.

⁵ So they reward me evil for good,

 and hatred for my love.

⁶ They say, "Appoint a wicked man against him;

 let an accuser stand on his right.

⁷ When he is tried, let him be found guilty;

 let his prayer be counted as sin.

⁸ May his days be few;

 may another seize his position.

⁹ May his children be orphans,

 and his wife a widow.

¹⁰ May his children wander about and beg;

 may they be driven out of the ruins they inhabit.

¹¹ May the creditor seize all that he has;

 may strangers plunder the fruits of his toil.

¹² May there be no one to do him a kindness,

 nor anyone to pity his orphaned children.

¹³ May his posterity be cut off;

 may his name be blotted out in the second generation.

¹⁴ May the iniquity of his father be remembered before the LORD,

 and do not let the sin of his mother be blotted out.

¹⁵ Let them be before the LORD continually,

 and may his memory be cut off from the earth.

¹⁶ For he did not remember to show kindness (*hesed*),

but pursued the poor and needy

and the brokenhearted to their death.

¹⁷ He loved to curse; let curses come on him.

He did not like blessing; may it be far from him.

¹⁸ He clothed himself with cursing as his coat,

may it soak into his body like water, like oil into his bones.

¹⁹ May it be like a garment that he wraps around himself,

like a belt that he wears every day."

²⁰ May that be the reward of my accusers from the LORD,

of those who speak evil against my life.

vav ²¹ But you, O LORD my Lord,

act on my behalf for your name's sake;

because your steadfast love (*hesed*) is good, deliver me.

²² For I am poor and needy,

and my heart is pierced within me.

²³ I am gone like a shadow at evening;

I am shaken off like a locust.

²⁴ My knees are weak through fasting;

my body has become gaunt.

²⁵ I am an object of scorn to my accusers;

when they see me, they shake their heads.

²⁶ Help me, O LORD my God!

Save me according to your steadfast love (*hesed*).

²⁷ Let them know that this is your hand;

you, O LORD, have done it.

²⁸ Let them curse, but you will bless.

Let my assailants be put to shame; may your servant be glad.

²⁹ May my accusers be clothed with dishonor;

may they be wrapped in their own shame as in a mantle.

30 With my mouth I will give great thanks to the LORD;

I will praise him in the midst of the throng.

31 For he stands at the right hand of the needy,

to save them from those who would condemn them to death.

PSALM 140 (NRSV)

Prayer for Deliverance from Enemies

TO THE LEADER. A PSALM OF DAVID.

1 Deliver me, O LORD, from evildoers;

protect me from those who are violent,

2 who plan evil things in their minds

and stir up wars continually.

3 They make their tongue sharp as a snake's,

and under their lips is the venom of vipers.   *Selah*

4 Guard me, O LORD, from the hands of the wicked;

protect me from the violent

who have planned my downfall.

5 The arrogant have hidden a trap for me,

and with cords they have spread a net,

along the road they have set snares for me.   *Selah*

6 I say to the LORD, "You are my God;

give ear, O LORD, to the voice of my supplications."

7 O LORD, my Lord, my strong deliverer,

you have covered my head in the day of battle.

8 Do not grant, O LORD, the desires of the wicked;

do not further their evil plot.   *Selah*

9 Those who surround me lift up their heads;

let the mischief of their lips overwhelm them!

¹⁰ Let burning coals fall on them!

    Let them be flung into pits, no more to rise!

¹¹ Do not let the slanderer be established in the land;

    let evil speedily hunt down the violent!

¹² I know that the LORD maintains the cause of the needy,

    and executes justice for the poor.

¹³ Surely the righteous shall give thanks to your name;

    the upright shall live in your presence.

PSALM 141 (NRSV)

Prayer for Preservation from Evil

A PSALM OF DAVID.

¹ I call upon you, O LORD; come quickly to me;

    give ear to my voice when I call to you.

² Let my prayer be counted as incense before you,

    and the lifting up of my hands as an evening sacrifice.

³ Set a guard over my mouth, O LORD;

    keep watch over the door of my lips.

⁴ Do not turn my heart to any evil,

    to busy myself with wicked deeds

in company with those who work iniquity;

    do not let me eat of their delicacies.

⁵ Let the righteous strike me;

    let the faithful correct me.

Never let the oil of the wicked anoint my head,

    for my prayer is continually against their wicked deeds.

⁶ When they are given over to those who shall condemn them,

    then they shall learn that my words were pleasant.

⁷ Like a rock that one breaks apart and shatters on the land,
  so shall their bones be strewn at the mouth of Sheol.

ᵛᵃᵛ ⁸ But my eyes are turned toward you, O GOD, my Lord;
  in you I seek refuge; do not leave me defenseless.
⁹ Keep me from the trap that they have laid for me,
  and from the snares of evildoers.
¹⁰ Let the wicked fall into their own nets,
  while I alone escape.

PSALM 143 (NRSV)

Prayer for Deliverance from Enemies
A PSALM OF DAVID.

¹ Hear my prayer, O LORD;
  give ear to my supplications in your faithfulness;
  answer me in your righteousness.
² Do not enter into judgment with your servant,
  for no one living is righteous before you.

³ For the enemy has pursued me,
  crushing my life to the ground,
  making me sit in darkness like those long dead.
⁴ Therefore my spirit faints within me;
  my heart within me is appalled.

⁵ I remember the days of old,
  I think about all your deeds,
  I meditate on the works of your hands.
⁶ I stretch out my hands to you;
  my soul thirsts for you like a parched land.   *Selah*

⁷ Answer me quickly, O LORD;
  my spirit fails.
Do not hide your face from me,
  or I shall be like those who go down to the Pit.
⁸ Let me hear of your steadfast love (*hesed*) in the morning,
  for in you I put my trust.
Teach me the way I should go,
  for to you I lift up my soul.

⁹ Save me, O LORD, from my enemies;
  I have fled to you for refuge.
¹⁰ Teach me to do your will,
  for you are my God.
Let your good spirit lead me
  on a level path.

¹¹ For your name's sake, O LORD, preserve my life.
  In your righteousness bring me out of trouble.
¹² In your steadfast love cut off my enemies,
  and destroy all my adversaries, for I am your servant.

APPENDIX F

BIBLIOGRAPHY

Allender, Dan. *The Hidden Hope in Lament.* Bainbridge Island, WA: *Mars Hill Review* 1, pp. 25-38. (1994)

Berrigan, Daniel. *Lamentations: From New York to Kabul and Beyond.* Chicago: Sheed and Ward, Chicago, 2002.

Brener, Anne. *Mourning and Mitzvah: A Guided Journal for Walking the Mourner's Path Through Grief to Healing.* Woodstock: Jewish Lights, 1997.

Brueggemann, Walter. *The Psalms: The Life of Faith.* Minneapolis: Fortress Press, 1995.

Brueggemann, Walter. *The Message of the Psalms.* Minneapolis: Augsburg, 1984.

Brueggemann, Walter. *The Threat of Life: Sermons on Pain, Power, and Weakness.* Minneapolis: Fortress, 1996.

Brueggemann, Walter. *Awed to Heaven, Rooted in Earth: Prayers of Walter Brueggemann.* Minneapolis: Fortress, 2003.

Carson, D. A. *Holy Sonnets of the Twentieth Century.* Grand Rapids: Baker, 1994.

Clark, Gordon R. *The Word Hesed in the Hebrew Bible. Journal for the Study of the Old Testament Supplement Series,* 157, Sheffield, 1993.

Crabb, Larry. *Shattered Dreams: God's Unexpected Pathway to Joy.* Colorado Springs: Waterbrook, 2001.

Floysvik, Ingvar. *When God Becomes My Enemy: The Theology of the Complaint Psalms.* St. Louis: Concordia Academic Press, 1997.

Gerstenberger, Erhard S. *Psalms, Part 2 and Lamentations, Volume XV, The Forms of Old Testament Literature.* Grand Rapids: Eerdmanns, 2001.

Heater, Homer. "Structure and Meaning in Lamentations." *BSac* 149:595 (July 92), p. 305.

Henderson, Frank. *Liturgies of Lament.* Chicago: Liturgy Training Publications, 1994.

Hsu, Albert Y. *Grieving a Suicide: A Loved One's Search for Comfort, Answers and Hope.* Downers Grove: InterVarsity Press, 2002.

Jinkins, Michael. *In the House of the Lord: Inhabiting the Psalms of Lament.* Collegeville, Minn.: The Liturgical Press, 1998.

Kidner, Derek. *Psalms: An Introduction and Commentary.* Downers Grove: Inter-Varsity Press, 1973.

Leithhart, Peter J. *From Silence to Song: The Davidic Liturgical Revolution.* Moscow, ID: Canon Press. Moscow, 2003.

Leon-Dufour, Xavier. *Dictionary of the New Testament.* New York: Harper and Row, 1980.

Lewis, C. S. *A Grief Observed.* New York: Bantam, 1980.

Moore, R. Kelvin. *The Psalms of Lamentation and the Enigma of Suffering,* Volume 50. Lewiston: Mellen Biblical Press, 1996.

Peterson, Eugene. *Leap Over a Wall.* San Francisco: Harper, 1997.

Sakenfeld, Katherine Doob. *The Meaning of Hesed in the Hebrew Bible: A New Inquiry.* Eugene: Wipf and Stock, 1978.

Seerveld, Calvin. *On Being Human.* Burlington, Ontario: Welch, 1988.

Seerveld, Calvin. "Reading and Hearing the Psalms: The Gut of the Bible," Pro Rege: 27:4 (June 1999): pp. 20-32.

Tileston, Mary W. editor "Great Souls at Prayer." Cambridge: James Clarke and Co, 1898.

Tsevat, Matitiahu. *The Meaning of the Book of Job.* Hebrew Union College Annual 37 pp. 73-106. (66)

Westermann, Claus. *Praise and Lament in the Psalms.* Atlanta: John Knox Press, 1981.

Westermann, Claus. *Lamentations: Issues and Interpretation.* Minneapolis: Fortress, 1994.

Wiesel, Elie. *Messengers of God.* New York: Summit Books, 1976.

Wiesel, Elie. *Five Biblical Portraits: Saul, Jonah, Jeremiah, Elijah and Joshua.* Notre Dame: University of Notre Dame Press, 1981.

Wiesel, Elie. *Messengers of God.* New York: Summit Books, 1976.

Wipf, Jane Larson. *A Fistful of Agates.* New York: Vantage, 2004.

Zuck, Roy B. editor. *Sitting with Job: Selected Studies on the Book of Job.* Grand Rapids: Baker, 1992.

NOTES

CHAPTER 4
1. *Ekah* is the Hebrew title of the book of Lamentations. It means "how."

CHAPTER 8
1. Job 15:13 (JPS); compare 34:36.
2. 16:1–17:16; 19:1-29; 21:1-34; 23:1–24:25.

CHAPTER 11
1. Compare Eliab's words to David in 1 Samuel 17:28.

CHAPTER 12
1. Compare Psalm 54 and 59; the superscriptions explain David's dilemma.
2. Compare Jeremiah 18:21.
3. Compare 1 Corinthians 5:5.
4. Compare Psalm 143:12.

CHAPTER 13
1. Michael Jinkins, *In the House of the Lord: Inhabiting the Psalms of Lament* (Collegeville, Minn.: The Liturgical Press, 1998), p. 120.
2. Compare Luke 1:59; 2:21.
3. Albert Y. Hsu, *Grieving a Suicide: A Loved One's Search for Comfort, Answers and Hope* (Downers Grove, Ill.: InterVarsity, 2002), p. 41.

CHAPTER 14
1. 1 Chronicles 29:29; 2 Chronicles 9:29.
2. 2 Samuel 6 and 1 Chronicles 13-16 describe David's role in bringing the ark back to Jerusalem and his leadership in reestablishing the worship of the Lord. The chronicler tells us he was responsible for the appointment of

"singers to sing joyful songs, accompanied by musical instruments: lyres, harps and cymbals" (1 Chronicles 15:16, NIV). Soon after that the details are made even more specific: "They were to play the lyres and the harps, Asaph was to sound the cymbals, and Benaiah and Jahaziel the priests were to blow the trumpets regularly before the ark of the covenant of God." (16:5-6, NIV) All this, apparently at David's direction.

In 16:7 we read a tantalizing hint, "That day David first committed to Asaph and his associates this psalm of thanks to the Lord." What follows is a magnificent inaugural hymn that opened a new era in the worship of Israel. We have seen that David's first real "job" was that of a musician (1 Sam. 16:14).

When we read the superscriptions that appear before roughly 117 of the 150 psalms and note that the majority of these include the phrase "of David," the fact becomes clear that he was the key figure not only in reorganizing worship but also composing the songs that were used in the new "ark-shrine" he built in his new capital, Jerusalem.

CHAPTER 15

1. Compare Paul's advice to the Corinthians in 1 Corinthians 7.
2. 23:33,34; Jeremiah 22:10-12; 2 Chronicles 36:1-4.
3. Compare Jeremiah 36:4-32.

CHAPTER 16

1. Elie Wiesel, *Messengers of God* (New York: Summit Books, 1976), p. 114.

CHAPTER 17

1. Acts 3:22; Hebrews 4:14.

CHAPTER 20

1. Davidic psalms with *hesed*: 5:7; 6:4; 13:5; 17:7; 18:50; 21:7; 23:6; 25:6; 25:7; 25:10; 6:3; 31:7; 31:16; 31:21; 32:10; 36:5; 36:7; 36:10; 40:10,11; 51:1; 52:1; 52:8; 57:3,10; 59:10,16; 61:7; 62:12; 63:3; 69:13,16; 86:5,13,15; 101:1; 103:4,8,11,17; 108:4; 109:21,26; 138:8; 143:8,12; 144:2; 145:8.

Some other key references: Exodus 33:19; Deuteronomy 13:17; 18:11,18; 30:3; 1 Samuel 20:14-17; 49:10; 2 Samuel 24:14; 1 Chronicles 16:4; Isaiah 14:1; 30:18; 49:10; 55:3; 54:8; Jeremiah 12:15; 33:26,42; Lamentations 3:22; Ezekiel 39:25; Micah 7:20,32; Daniel 9:9,18; Micah 7:19; Habakkuk 3:2; Nehemiah 9:27—28; 13:22; Jeremiah 31:19.

CHAPTER 21

1. Outline of relevant passages from the Gospels:

John 1: The Word becomes flesh. If John had a specific "word" in mind perhaps it was not logos but *hesed*. "Full of grace and truth . . ."

Matthew 5; Luke 6:21: The Beatitudes, a barocha for those who mourn.

Matthew 5; Luke 6:27: Love for enemies, a definition of *hesed*.

Matthew 10:35: Jesus quotes from a lament in Micah 7 to explain His mission.

John 11:35: Jesus weeps when Mary comes to get Him. Verse 38: "deeply moved" at the tomb of Lazarus.

Matthew 24:37-9; Luke 13:34: Jesus laments for Jerusalem, "O Jerusalem . . ." Sounds like Jeremiah lamenting before the first destruction of Jerusalem. Also comes after the seven woes, a prophetic utterance as well.

Luke 19:41-44: When Jesus laments over the destruction that is coming to Jerusalem, He sounds surprisingly like Jeremiah, who foresaw the first destruction of the Temple. After all, there were some who confused Jesus as another Jeremiah: "When Jesus came to the region of Caesarea Philippi, he asked his disciples, 'Who do people say the Son of Man is?' They replied, 'Some say John the Baptist; others say Elijah; and still others, Jeremiah or one of the prophets.'" (Matthew 16:13-14).

Jesus weeps loudly over Jerusalem. Jesus then enters the temple and quotes Jeremiah! (It is not as if Jesus could have "lamented" once and for all in some kind of neat timeline. At least twice, and probably several times more, He overflows with grief for the city and the people He loves.

Matthew 26:36; Mark 14: Gethsemane "soul overwhelmed to the point of death." The overwhelmed soul of Jesus. He struggles with His will against God's, never lets go.

Matthew 27:45: Crucifixion. "My God, my God, why have You forsaken me?" Psalm 22.

CHAPTER 23

1. See also Acts 3:19; Colossians 2:14; Revelation 3:5.